REMEMBERING McDONOUGH COUNTY

JOHN E. HALLWAS

THE History PRESS

Published by The History Press
Charleston, SC 29403
www.historypress.net

First published 2009

All images are courtesy of Archives and Special Collections at Western Illinois University Libraries unless otherwise noted.

Manufactured in the United States

ISBN 978.1.59629.838.5

Library of Congress Cataloging-in-Publication Data

Hallwas, John E.
Remembering Mcdonough County / John E. Hallwas.
p. cm.
ISBN 978-1-59629-838-5
1. McDonough County (Ill.)--History--Anecdotes. 2. McDonough County (Ill.)--Biography--Anecdotes. I. Title.
F547.M13H36 2009
977.3'42--dc22
2009040838

Dedicated to my granddaughter,
Emily Hallwas,
an avid reader and committed writer
who is keeping her own memories of McDonough County.

Contents

Preface	7
Introduction	9
Part I: People Who Deeply Belonged	
Pioneers with Long Memories	15
Quintus Walker: Deer Hunter and Storyteller	21
Early Historian S.J. Clarke	25
"The Lost Child" and Forgotten Female Rememberers	29
W.H. Hainline and a Culture of Memory	33
C.V. Chandler: Macomb as a Meaningful Place	39
Alexander McLean: Leader and Historian	45
James Burns and the Culture of History	49
Alex Holmes and the Personal Past	53
Quincy Hainline, the Old Storyteller	59
Bushnell Poet Marian Stearns Curry	63
Martha K. Graham: Teacher and Writer	69
Don O'Harra: Last of the Old-Time Country Printers	75
Part II: Places in the Heart	
Dealing with Death: The Old Macomb Cemetery	83
Pennington Point: The Old Days in a Rural Hamlet	87
Hills Grove and Rattlesnake Den Hollow	91
The Legendary Place Called Gin Ridge	97

The Old Fairground and the Times that Were 103
Colchester's Pleasant Valley—and Ragtown 109
Vishnu Springs: Resort Town and Wildlife Sanctuary 115
Memories and Ghost Stories of Scott's Church and Cemetery 121
The Gooseneck Neighborhood and Its Famous Ghost 127
Western's Nature Area, the Ravine, and Its Theater 133
The Wilds of Crooked Creek 139

Preface

This book includes some previously published items that have been revised for the present collection, but most of the content has been written for *Remembering McDonough County.* The biographical sketches of Quintus Walker, S.J. Clarke, and C.V. Chandler, as well as the accounts of the Old Macomb Cemetery, Gin Ridge, Vishnu Springs, and the Gooseneck Ghost, appeared almost thirty years ago in my *Macomb Journal* column called "Our Regional Heritage," and they were subsequently included in my collection called *McDonough County Heritage* (1984), which has long been out of print. Again, all of those items have been revised. Previously published in the *Macomb Eagle* in more recent years, for the "Images of the Past" column, are the accounts of Pennington Point and Colchester's Pleasant Valley. They have also been revised for this collection. The biographical sketch of printer Don O'Harra first appeared as a *Macomb Journal* commentary piece in 2009 and has been expanded for inclusion here.

Of course, this volume is indebted to a variety of county histories, to my 1990 book *Macomb: A Pictorial History* (now out of print), and to the *McDonough County Historical Society Newsletter.* But the most important sources are the McDonough County newspapers, which are available on microfilm at Archives and Special Collections, Western Illinois University Library. A still useful bibliographic essay devoted to a broad range of sources for those interested in McDonough County history is printed at the close of my *McDonough County Heritage.*

The photographs for this illustrated volume are, for the most part, courtesy of Archives and Special Collections at the WIU Library. My appreciation is extended to the manager of that sizable collection of historical photographs, Kathy Nichols, who helped to select the visuals for this book. I also wish to thank John Graham of Western Illinois University and Judy Ashton of the Bushnell Historical Society, who provided photographs.

Nichols, who has a superb knowledge of Macomb's history and a peerless acquaintance with local newspaper files, was also indispensable with the research for this volume, and she critiqued a draft of the manuscript. She epitomizes the great truth that all worthwhile knowledge of the past requires caring.

My appreciation as well is extended to Julie Foster, managing editor of The History Press, who was very helpful through the various stages of the publishing process, and senior editor Hilary McCullough.

Finally, my thanks go as well to my wife Garnette, a Macomb native who has shared her insights into the people of McDonough County for over forty years, and who adapted to my tight writing schedule during the months when this book was being written.

Introduction

For well over forty years, I have been interested in the heritage of Macomb and McDonough County. As a non-local student who came to Western Illinois University in the early 1960s, I was struck by the sense of heritage on Macomb's courthouse square and in Chandler Park. At WIU itself, I sensed the tension between vast expansion, as the campus developed northward through an unprecedented construction effort, and the traditional look and feel of Sherman Hall, the "Old Main" building, where students like myself still took classes, met with professors, and even attended an occasional program in the auditorium. Just east of Lincoln Tower, the new high-rise residence hall where I lived as a freshman, was the old ravine, with its paths worn by generations of students and its then unused outdoor amphitheater. There was a sense of tradition, too, about Morgan Gym, with its basketball games and dances, and the lab school, Simpkins Hall, where would-be teachers like myself had learned their trade since the 1930s.

I was also curious enough about the local past to visit the basement of Memorial Library, where the small number of local history books were shelved, and locate a copy of S.J. Clarke's 1878 *History of McDonough County*. Reading in it there, I was especially impressed by the author's vivid accounts of the Underground Railroad and the coming of the Civil War. I was probably the only WIU student of my era who strolled through Oakwood Cemetery and noted the gravestones of some figures from Clarke's history—James M. Campbell, William H. Randolph, C.V. Chandler, and others.

An early teacher, mentor, and friend was Professor Alfred J. Lindsey, who was deeply rooted in Macomb, as well as a Western graduate, and he seemed to know everything about everyone—from former president Frank Beu and legendary coach Ray Hanson to newspaperwoman Lida Crabb and auctioneer Hughey Martin. He had a profound sense of place. My 1966 marriage to a Macomb girl also promoted my involvement with, and knowledge of, local life; and my part-time jobs at old businesses like Scott's Pharmacy (located in a building constructed in 1872) and the Lamoine Hotel (which had served as a community center since 1927) sharpened my awareness of local heritage.

Those who know me well realize that I am a very purpose-driven individual who senses in our time the decline of community, the fading of social commitment, the erosion of meaningful engagement with place, the diminishing connection with earlier generations, and the loss of culturally significant stories—and who struggles against these related problems. I speak and write almost obsessively about the local past because, for us in the present day, to acquaint ourselves with earlier residents, to share an awareness of what happened many years ago, and to realize the forces that have shaped our culture promotes community and fosters a sense of belonging. It draws local people together, profoundly impacting their communal or social identity, and hence their willingness to participate, appreciate, and contribute.

Remembering McDonough County is not just another book that recounts the past in an interesting place. It also examines the lives of individuals who did remember and who lived deep, meaningful lives in McDonough County as reflectors and expressers of local culture. In a sense, they are all my forebears, and this is a profoundly personal book. Spiritually, figures like Quintus Walker, W.H. Hainline, and Martha K. Graham are the polar opposite of the outcast and pursued Maxwell brothers in my recent book, *Dime Novel Desperadoes*. As my section title here says, they "Deeply Belonged." They remind us that a place like McDonough County becomes important to us, and helps to center our lives, because of the stories that we accumulate about it, the local people we know, and our memories of our own experience there. And such a place, absorbed into the self, can have profound spiritual impact. As French thinker and writer Simone Weil once put it, "To be rooted is perhaps the most important and least recognized need of the human soul."

In other words, the local past is ultimately a psychological reality, which can be rich and meaningful or shallow and meaningless, depending on the quality of our inner lives. And thus, people of the past, the local dead, are either inconsequential strangers, unknown and unrelated to us, or significant spiritual ancestors who deepen our own experience and help us become rooted. Each of us makes that choice.

This book also depicts places that have vanished or are no longer vital to the culture of McDonough County—a historic but seldom-visited cemetery, a mill site that became a park, the old county fairground, and various ghost towns, rural neighborhoods, and wild places. Each of them is not just a reflection of cultural change but a case study of the reciprocity between people and a particular place. The challenge is not just to know the facts about a certain location but to realize the meaning of that place for the people who interacted with it. And as long as those locations are remembered, or re-created in local history and literature, they still function as cultural anchors. They contribute to the uniqueness, the distinction, the complex spiritual essence of McDonough County, which impacts the lives of those who live there.

For readers who do not reside in McDonough County, this book is an opportunity to become acquainted with yet another version of the mythic American experience of cultural creation—to know another facet of the Midwestern heritage through photographs and stories, memories and meanings, all derived from an ordinary place that became extraordinary for the people who lived there and called it home.

Part I
People Who Deeply Belonged

Pioneers with Long Memories

Many early residents of McDonough County lived long enough to find that their recollections of frontier life, conveyed through oral stories, newspaper articles, or history books, were of real interest to their contemporaries. In fact, from the post–Civil War years through the first few decades of the twentieth century, there was a strong culture of memory in the county. The recollected past was important.

That developed because there had been so much cultural change since the pioneer (or pre-railroad) days and because the Civil War that came shortly after the Northern Cross Railroad had arrived was a watershed in local and national life—something to be recalled, pondered, regretted, marked, and celebrated. Also, as the decades continued, the early settlers—the people who had come in the late 1820s, 1830s, and 1840s—were vanishing one by one, and their experience seemed essential for local identity.

Fortunately, one of the earliest and most important pioneers left some brief recollections. James Clarke arrived with his wife Mary (always called "Polly") and their six children in March 1830. Like so many early settlers in the county, they were Kentuckians. Individualism and hospitality were important values; hunting and storytelling were popular activities. Kinship was cherished—and soon six of Clarke's brothers and sisters also settled in the county. Clarke was elected county commissioner and also became a justice of the peace. He had a log home in Chalmers Township, two miles from the designated county seat, but he later built a double log house in Macomb, at the corner of West Jackson Street and the square, which was an early tavern (or hotel) and meeting place.

In December 1874, when he was seventy-seven years old and was the most revered pioneer except for fellow Kentuckian James M. Campbell, Clarke was interviewed by the editor of the *Macomb Eagle*, who was awed by him because he "possessed a memory which could reach back to the trials, tribulations, and adventures of the early days of this locality." Indeed, Clarke recalled the organizing of the county, in which he had played a key role. In fact, the first county court was held in August 1830 "under an elm tree" on his property, and at the end of that year he was appointed to ride to Springfield to purchase at the land office the 149½ acres on which Macomb would soon be laid out. Clarke also revealed that Circuit Court Judge Richard M. Young, of Galena, "named the county seat Macomb" and recruited James M. Campbell to go there as the first circuit clerk and lay out the town. Clarke was, then, a kind of authenticating voice who could verify from his own experience the start of local government and the creation of the county seat.

He could also verify the pioneer struggle. In a letter to his nephew, S.J. Clarke, which was published in a local magazine called *Clarke's Monthly* during 1876, he vividly recalled the legendary "winter of the deep snow." In fact, the three-day storm that brought it on caught him returning from Springfield, on his errand to establish the county seat, and he almost didn't make it back. Although he did not celebrate himself for doing that, his founding effort became a kind of heroic deed, worthy of remembrance by the other pioneers. His account also reveals the grim struggle for survival that followed his return:

> *The snow fell to an average depth of about four feet and remained on the ground for about three months. All kinds of wild game literally starved to death….*
>
> *I did not have my corn gathered, and had a good sized family to feed…. Each day we would have to go out to the field, and where we could see a stalk of corn standing above the snow, reach down until we came to an ear, and pull it off, gathering enough for the day. There were no mills in the county, and each family would, with a mortar and pestle, pound their corn so as to make bread* [flour]…. *This, with what game we could get, was what we had to live on during the long winter.*
>
> *Several families* [had come] *to the county that fall and, of course, had no corn. All things were then held more than in common. Those that had none were welcome to help themselves from their more fortunate neighbors, all that was required of them being that they should gather it themselves.*

This 1835 log cabin built north of Macomb by James Clarke is similar to the log "tavern" that he had constructed earlier on the east side of the square.

So Clarke's account of that initial winter becomes a kind of mythic story of pioneer fortitude, as well as a parable of survival through sharing. It would be hard to find the story of another American county that begins with a more desperate ordeal. Several other early pioneers also recalled "the horrors of that long winter," as James W. Brattle put it, but none validated the heroic pioneer experience quite like Clarke did.

Of course, the most common topic for pioneer reminiscence was early Macomb. After all, it had changed the most over many decades, from a log cabin hamlet to a village of small frame shops with a square brick courthouse, and finally to a railroad shipping point with many two-story brick buildings and, by 1872, a magnificent courthouse. And it was the social, commercial, political, governmental, and, later, educational axis of McDonough County, a kind of sacred center that unified local culture. The placement of the courthouse square in the county's exact center promoted that significance, as did Macomb rituals like Fourth of July celebrations at Liberty Grove and, later, Memorial Day observances at Oakwood Cemetery.

A fine brief account of the early county seat appeared in 1897, in a newspaper article of recollections by Anderson Cannon, who was then seventy-six years old. Of course, by then Macomb had mostly brick two-story business buildings and about three thousand people, so the log cabin village was hard for locals to imagine. And most of the pioneers were gone. The opening to this newspaper article memoir reflects the relationship between remaining pioneers, regarded as heroic culture-makers, and the townspeople. Cannon obviously enjoyed the role of venerated storyteller—and the term "Uncle" was, in fact, a title of affectionate respect:

> *Uncle Anderson Cannon was one of McDonough County's pioneers. He possesses a remarkable memory of early events and loves to recount his experiences….*
>
> *"I arrived at the hamlet of Macomb on Oct. 27, 1833. There were at that time eight log buildings and the courthouse. I remember the name of every man in town at that time…. The courthouse stood on the corner now occupied by Venard's bookstore. After they…got a better one, Edward Dyer bought the old* [log] *one and used it for a wagon shop….*
>
> *"Just south of the courthouse, on the opposite corner* [of the square], *Abe and Sol Dover kept a saloon (grocery we called it then). Whisky was cheap then, 25 cents a pint or a picayune (5 cents) a dram. Jonathan Baker kept a sort of grocery down west of where Blount's lumber yard now is.*
>
> *"James Clarke kept the tavern* [i.e., hotel]. *It stood where Smith's hardware store now stands. The tavern was the finest building in town. The logs were hewn. The rest of the buildings were just rough poles….*
>
> *"Jim Campbell built the first house with glass windows. The others just had a couple of logs cut out and a cloth hung over the opening, so when a fellow wanted to shoot a deer or a prairie wolf, he just raised the cloth and banged away.*
>
> *"My father located southwest of town on a piece of brush land. We had an ox team, a wooden mole-board plow, and a wooden-tooth harrow. I tell you,* [making a farm] *was tough work."*

Cannon mentions a number of local touchstones: the first (log) courthouse, the pioneer businessmen, James Clarke, and James Campbell—as well as the heroic making of a prairie farm. The overall impression is of a compact, and comprehensible, local world, where the men, at least, all knew one another.

Various other pioneer recollections mention the coming of frame buildings, the 1834 brick courthouse, notable early hotels and stores, and the local pork-packing industry, but a particularly interesting memoir-letter by James Laughlin, published in 1922, characterizes some local people and

The first brick courthouse in Macomb, constructed in 1834, where pioneers gathered and drank whisky on the lawn during election day. An 1860s photograph.

problems of the 1840s—and includes a sketch of Anderson Cannon that explains why he had also referred to the price of whisky:

> *To begin with, I think of Isaac Grantham, the county clerk, noted for his quiet demeanor and pleasant manners.... James M. Campbell was the circuit clerk, known for his rough manners and* [for being] *as profane as the Old Scratch himself.... N.P. Tinsley, merchant and pork packer on the north side,* [was a] *fine business man; kept his own counsel, bought and sold to get gain....*
>
> *In the early day a family by the name of Cannon lived on East Jackson Street, not far from the square, of whom the quaint hero, Anderson Cannon, was one. He was a Whig all over and lost no opportunity to denounce the Democrats. He would often drink too much, but whiskey was cheap then.*
>
> *On election day, when the whole county voted in Macomb, it was a common thing to have a barrel of whisky in the courthouse yard and the head knocked out* [i.e., opened], *and tin cups hanging around so everyone could help himself. And the result was often a fistfight, with bare knuckles. Blood flowed freely, and the two men would be a sight to behold when the fight was over....*
>
> *That brings us to the scourge of cholera* [in 1849–51]*—a fearful, tearful time. With William Foster and Sammy Fox, Father* [Theodore Laughlin, a carpenter] *could not make coffins fast enough;* [they were] *just rough boxes. Your humble servant would take a box in a wagon to where someone had died, put the corpse in the box, close the lid, and send it to the cemetery, only to go over the same thing again and again.*

Laughlin, who was eighty-five in 1922, mentions that he knew personally the people whom he recalled, and that his written recollection was an effort "to stand them up before us and take a long last farewell look at them." He realized that the pioneer past anchored him and others to the culture of McDonough County—and that he was perhaps the last man who could remember well the people of the 1840s. As long as he remained, they were the still living, reachable components of the town's beginning. He could depict them, "stand them up," and share them with local residents who had come later.

A pioneer with a special sense of connection to Macomb's early days, Laughlin died in 1927. And the people of his boyhood era were finally gone.

Quintus Walker: Deer Hunter and Storyteller

One of the most widely known and well-liked McDonough County pioneers was Quintus Walker, a Kentucky-bred frontiersman whose skill as a deer hunter was legendary, partly because he was also renowned as a storyteller. His love for wildlife also led to the establishment of a deer park that became a kind of early tourist site—and a link with the pioneer past.

Quintus was born in Adair County, Kentucky, on May 20, 1814. His father was Alexander Walker, who had brought his family from Rockbridge County, Virginia, to that location twenty years earlier. At that time, the elder Walker was married to Mary Harmon. Before she died in 1811, they had eleven children, including Cyrus, who later became a noted lawyer and politician. In 1812, Alexander married a widow, Margaret F. Coumbs, and they had three more children, the eldest of whom was Quintus.

In 1830, some of the Walkers, including teenage Quintus, moved with a neighboring family, the Campbells, to Clary's Grove, Illinois, the earliest settlement in Menard County. It was just west of New Salem, where Lincoln would arrive the following spring. A year later, the Walkers and Campbells moved again, to McDonough County. They built a log cabin near Camp Creek.

On August 4, 1833, Quintus, then nineteen, married Mahala Campbell, and they took a "wedding tour," which he later recalled in one of his stories of pioneer life, printed in the 1885 county history:

> *I took the four wheels of a wagon, put a sack of corn on, and hitched a yoke of oxen to it, and we seated ourselves on the sack, driving the cattle without*

> *any lines. There being no road, we struck off across the prairie to Bacon's mill, below Macomb. On the way we stopped on Troublesome Creek, to see the Indian's grave who had been killed by a deer. He was buried in a trough on top of the ground, and a pen of poles was built around, with loop holes cut in it for him to shoot through. His gun, knife, kettle, etc. were also placed in the pen, but they had been stolen* [by the time] *we saw it.*

A few other pioneers also remembered that Indian grave, and various folkloric stories developed to depict the man's death. Quintus may have been fascinated with the grave site and the stories because he was already an avid deer hunter. In fact, for the young Kentuckian there was a certain mystique about deer.

Two years later, Quintus and Mahala moved to the almost uninhabited Walnut Grove Township, in northern McDonough County, where he became the most accomplished deer hunter in the area—and probably in all of western Illinois. By the time he was seventy, he estimated that he had killed more than one thousand deer—which suggests, of course, that something beyond the need for food was driving his exploits as a hunter. A superb tracker and a fine marksman, he recalled that "at one time I killed 10 deer in 11 successive shots." At a time when hunting prowess was an important basis for masculine stature, that kind of skill made Quintus Walker a renowned figure—the Davy Crockett of local pioneers.

And he was an accomplished narrator of his hunting adventures. The very detail that he provided stamped them as genuine accounts, rather than Crockett-type tall tales, as the following story of heroic defense by his highly trained hunting dog reveals:

> *My dog* [a young bull pup] *I had trained to creep close behind me. I got close enough so I could see the horns of one of the deer, and then I prepared to shoot.... I raised my gun and fired, and he dropped down. I felt sure I had hit him in the brain and, dropping my gun in the snow, I drew my knife and ran up to stick him, and placing one foot on the down horn, and grasping the other with one hand, I was about to stick him, when he sprang up, pushing against me as he did so, for a fight. I found I could not hold him down, so I called my dog, who sprang at the deer, grasping him by the throat. While the dog and deer were hotly engaged, I ran back to my gun and commenced to load, when I found that the snow had run into* [the chamber] *so I could not fire it, and while the dog and deer were fighting, I was trying to dry the gun so I*

> *could use it. They fought fiercely, and sometimes the deer would throw the dog as high as my head. They kept moving down the hill, but before I could get my gun in order to shoot, the dog became exhausted and the deer pushed him into a snowbank, and he lay there panting, too weak to renew the battle. The deer stood, and looked at him and me a minute, and then turning, ran off. I suppose that the* [rifle] *ball struck him at the base of the horn and only stunned him, and I have always believed that if it had not been for the dog, the buck would have killed me….*
>
> *The dog and I were both green at that time, and it taught us a lesson.*

The story is similar in some ways to the climactic fight in William Faulkner's masterpiece "The Bear," in which a young hunting dog that exemplifies courage takes on a great, relentlessly hunted creature, whose "wild and invincible spirit" has a lasting impact on a young hunter who cannot, or does not, fire his gun. No wonder Quintus Walker was a renowned storyteller, for this is a riveting and unforgettable tale.

As time went by, Walker's respect for the wild creatures he hunted prompted him to erect a large deer park at his homestead in Section 16, where he eventually had a breeding population that became semi-tamed. Fellow pioneer William T. Brooking described it in a memoir: "He had a park with a high fence in which he had about fifteen deer. The fence was made of rails set on end. He would frequently let his tame deer out in the cornfield, and they would return to the enclosure at night." What did the huge park, where deer "gamboled…contented and happy," as Walker put it, and where he raised many a motherless fawn, reveal about the renowned hunter? Love for the largest wild creatures in the county? A sense of environmental appreciation? His own version of Eden?

The deer park, which also had wild turkeys, geese, guinea fowls, and even young wolves for a time, soon became widely known. John Regan's *Emigrant's Guide to the Western States of America* (1852) describes it, and people came from many places just to see it. In fact, the Walker homestead eventually became known as Deer Park Farm. As late as 1895, the *Macomb Journal* reported that over two hundred people attended the sixtieth wedding anniversary of Quintus and Mahala Walker in "the noted Deer Park grove on their farm." On that occasion, Quintus spoke about his life on the frontier, and one can only imagine the response of his listeners in that celebrated place as the old, bearded icon of the frontier told them how it was then.

Quintus and Mahala Walker, who had been born a few days apart, in May 1814, became the longest-surviving pioneer couple in McDonough

Quintus and Mahala Walker with her brothers, David Campbell, John Campbell, and Sam Campbell, behind them, at the turn of the century.

County, symbolizing for younger generations the heroic era of settlement and struggle. And they died in the same year, 1902. Unfortunately, we know little about Mahala, but the surviving short memoir by Quintus and the accounts of him by several others who knew him, and were fascinated with him, make Quintus Walker one of the most intriguing local frontiersmen. A peerless hunter, he was also McDonough County's first renowned storyteller.

Early Historian S.J. Clarke

In 1878, S.J. Clarke of Macomb published his *History of McDonough County*. In the more than 130 years since that time, his book has become familiar to many people interested in the county's heritage—including myself, who first read some of his chapters when I was a college student. Yet even those who most admire and appreciate "Clarke's History," as it is commonly called, usually know nothing at all about the author, and most assume that he was an older man, remembering people and events of the past that he had known.

Because I share so many of his commitments and he is a kind of spiritual ancestor of mine in the social web of McDonough County, battling against forgetfulness and searching for cultural significance, I have been dedicated for many years to uncovering the details of his life story, which includes a remarkable achievement in history publishing.

S.J. Clarke was the son of David and Eliza Clarke, who were married in Green County, Kentucky, in 1825. They moved to McDonough County in 1830, arriving on November 15 with their two children. They had been encouraged to come by David's brother, James, who had settled near the place that was soon to be called Macomb in the spring of that same year. In fact, it was S.J.'s Uncle James who rode to Springfield at the end of 1830 to enter the quarter section of land on which Macomb was laid out the following spring.

David Clarke first settled in Chalmers Township, but he later sold that land and moved closer to the hamlet of Macomb. Although a farmer

Lithograph of historian and publisher S.J. Clarke, created in about 1920.

throughout his life, he was also appointed constable of McDonough County in 1832 and was later a justice of the peace. Like his older brother, he also operated a tavern (or hotel). A typical Kentuckian, he revered Andrew Jackson, voted Democratic, participated in camp meetings, drank whisky (in his early years), and—as his obituary says—"dearly loved to tell a good story…and could listen to one with equal pleasure."

After he injured himself while intoxicated, early in 1841, David Clarke became "a radical temperance man," as his son later put it. His anti-drinking views had a lifelong impact on S.J., and so did his interest in storytelling and his deep sense of belonging to the community.

S.J. (Samuel James) Clarke was born in 1842. When he was in his early teens, he started working as a printer's devil for the *Macomb Enterprise* (later called the *Macomb Journal*), which was published by T.S. Clarke (a cousin) and D.G. Swan. The newspaper office was located on the south side of the square, and by 1859 young S.J. was selling newspapers and magazines there and referred to himself as "a dealer in periodicals." Just seventeen, he was Macomb's youngest businessman.

For unknown reasons, Clarke did not serve in the Civil War. In the early 1860s, he started a bookstore on the north side of the square. He sold schoolbooks, children's books, newspapers, magazines, and stationery. The enterprise was made possible by a financial partnership with a relative, Charles P. Whitten.

After the war, Clarke married Harriet (Hattie) Martin, on New Year's Day 1867. Fascinated with books, he also started the Macomb Literary Society and became its first president, and he participated in plays put on by a local theater group. In the late 1860s, he wrote a comedy called *When Doctors Disagree, Who Shall Decide?* According to Alex Holmes, it was inspired by a local situation—a reported case of smallpox that left Macomb physicians in a controversy until "older ladies of the neighborhood, who had raised families, got together and…decided it was chickenpox." Holmes, who also acted in plays, called it "well written, acted, and received." It was, in any case, the first locally written play produced in McDonough County.

Early in 1868, Clarke and Whitten launched a biweekly newspaper called the *Western Light*. It was devoted to literature, art, science, local news, and the cause of temperance. Whitten left the business after four months, so Clarke published the *Western Light* alone until it failed at the end of that year.

Then he moved to Lincoln, Nebraska, where he ran a bookstore until the early 1870s. After he returned to Macomb, perhaps to help care for his ailing parents, S.J. launched a cultural and historical magazine called *Clarke's Monthly*, which carried some reminiscences of pioneer life in the county. It appeared in 1875 or 1876 and was evidently of short duration.

By that time, Clarke was already at work on his *History of McDonough County*. As he knew, short accounts of the county's early years had appeared in the *Macomb Eagle* (February 16; March 2, 16; April 6, 1861) and the *Macomb Journal* (August 13, 1869). Lawyer and Civil War veteran L.A. Simmons wrote the second of those, but the four-part first one is anonymous. Both were devoid of personal recollections.

Clarke made significant use of public records, but the distinguishing mark of his book was the successful incorporation of oral sources. As he said just after it was completed, "Many days and nights have I spent in listening to the stories of the old pioneers." Among the early settlers whom he interviewed were his Uncle James, who died in 1876; his mother, who died in 1877; and his father, who died in 1884.

As a result of his extensive use of pioneer recollections, Clarke created an uncommonly readable and interesting volume of local history. His chapters on "Personal Incidents and Anecdotes" and "The Underground Railroad," among others, display his interest in storytelling, while the section on "First Impressions" reveals his diligence in seeking a wide range of pioneer commentaries. He surely knew more older residents than anyone else of his generation, and his book was a quest for connection with them.

During the 1880s, Clarke became interested in the historical publishing business. As a result, he spent much time traveling in Iowa as a representative for a company in that field. In 1890, he moved to Chicago, where he established the S.J. Clarke Publishing Company. The firm specialized in county histories that were compilations of biographical sketches, and during the next few decades, Clarke published scores of them, especially for counties in Illinois, Iowa, Ohio, and Wisconsin. He later included narrative accounts too, and he also published city and state histories, such as Josiah S. Currey's

Chicago: Its History and Its Builders (1912) and Milo M. Quaife's *Wisconsin, the Progressive State* (1924).

Clarke was very successful as a publisher, and he became a rather wealthy man. He served as president of the firm for forty years, until he died in May 1930 at age eighty-eight. A few years prior to his death, he had moved to the fashionable suburb of Oak Park, where he and Hattie were eventually buried.

So, when "Clarke's History" appeared in 1878, the author was only thirty-seven, and it was a young man's expression of love and admiration for the pioneers of his parents' generation. That book was also the first title in a huge contribution to historical publishing. Perhaps no one in the history of the Midwest helped more people, in more places, remember.

"The Lost Child" and Forgotten Female Rememberers

As every local historian knows, women are much harder to track than men. Until recent generations, they were not business owners, political officeholders, cultural leaders, or heroic soldiers. They seldom made the newspapers. But their lives, too, were often remarkable, and some have been talented rememberers of the local past, although in fact, they have ironically been forgotten.

The earliest female writer about McDonough County's past was a young woman named Imogene Updegraff, who was born in Macomb in 1849. Her father was Joseph P. Updegraff, who had come from Ohio in 1833 to do the brickwork on the new courthouse. He later was a grocer for many years and served three terms as the mayor of Macomb. Little is known about Imogene's early life, but she was in the first graduating class (1868) at Macomb High School, where she received high honors, and she also attended Lombard College in Galesburg. From 1869 to 1874, she wrote various essays for the *Macomb Journal*, often criticizing "modern" shallow culture. They all appeared under a male pseudonym, "Gene Graff."

Like S.J. Clarke, she had heard stories about early life in the county from her parents. One that particularly interested her was the stressful, four-day search for a lost child in the wilds of Walnut Grove Township, which occurred in August 1834. Her father had been one of the searchers, so she had one dependable source, but she clearly asked other older people for their memories as well.

Her lengthy account, "The Lost Child: Reminiscences of Forty years Ago," appeared in three installments in the 1874 *Macomb Journal*, under her familiar pseudonym. It was unlike anything else she had written, and it created a sensation, for older county residents recalled the episode and were excited to have the details, while younger people felt swept back into a very different time.

Despite her subtitle, "The Lost Child" is far more than "Reminiscences," for Updegraff dramatized the historical information that she had accumulated, creating a kind of plot-driven, thematically unified, nonfictional narrative. The story is not only set back in time but also back on the uncivilized frontier, when "McDonough County was a wild and almost uninhabited region." Yet in the author's account, that era in the county stands opposed to modern culture, for it is devoted to what has since been slipping away: unselfish commitment to others, a sense of real community. As she says, "Our little city, with her lofty spires, substantial buildings, pretty houses, and all her convenience for work and recreation, then consisted of a few log cabins, a store, a shop, and a handful of happy, contented people. Happy—because sectarianism, fashion [i.e., social status], and avarice had not then shriveled their souls."

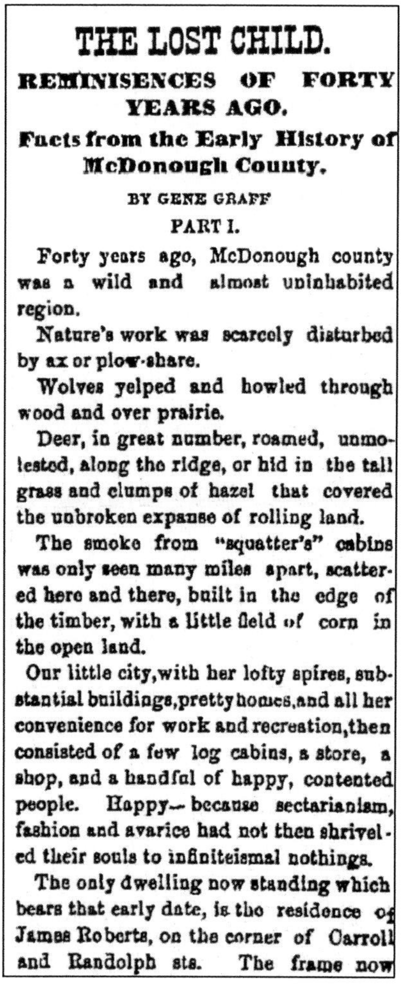

THE LOST CHILD.

REMINISENCES OF FORTY YEARS AGO.

Facts from the Early History of McDonough County.

BY GENE GRAFF

PART I.

Forty years ago, McDonough county was a wild and almost uninhabited region.

Nature's work was scarcely disturbed by ax or plow-share.

Wolves yelped and howled through wood and over prairie.

Deer, in great number, roamed, unmolested, along the ridge, or hid in the tall grass and clumps of hazel that covered the unbroken expanse of rolling land.

The smoke from "squatter's" cabins was only seen many miles apart, scattered here and there, built in the edge of the timber, with a little field of corn in the open land.

Our little city, with her lofty spires, substantial buildings, pretty homes, and all her convenience for work and recreation, then consisted of a few log cabins, a store, a shop, and a handful of happy, contented people. Happy— because sectarianism, fashion and avarice had not then shriveled their souls to infiniteismal nothings.

The only dwelling now standing which bears that early date, is the residence of James Roberts, on the corner of Carroll and Randolph sts. The frame now

"The Lost Child" serial by Imogene Updegraff fascinated local readers when it appeared in the 1874 *Macomb Journal*.

As that suggests, the story celebrates those pioneers, who turned out in remarkable numbers when the word spread that a preschool child of Ephraim Palmer, little Willie, had wandered off into the woods along Crooked Creek and couldn't be located. The volunteers from Macomb constituted a virtual who's who of the town's early leaders: "Col. William Bailey, James M. Campbell, James Clarke, David Clarke, J.L. Russell, J.W. Westfall, Thompson Chandler, Charles

Chandler, J.L. Anderson, and J.P. Updegraff [the author's father]." Others came from Job's Settlement, Carter's Settlement, and more distant points as well. As she puts it, "The whole [county-wide] community was aroused."

In the present-tense narrative, as the first day turns up no sign of the child and two more fruitless, exhausting days follow, the searchers cover the entire northwest quarter of the county, and they begin to despair of finding the child alive in a wilderness that was, after all, still inhabited by wolves that "howled through the woods and over the prairies." Meanwhile, the child's mother is overcome with anxiety and fatigue, and as the first installment closes, she virtually collapses, moaning, "O My child! My precious Willie! Where is he? Have the wolves torn him to pieces? Has my little boy drowned? Go look for him again! My God, I shall go wild!" This dramatic account of the woman's emotional breakdown surely reveals Updegraff's imaginative recreation of the way in which Willie's mother was affected by the ordeal—and it shows the female insight that makes this riveting historical account unique.

The story has a happy ending, for on the fourth exhausting day of searching in the August heat, men working down from the headwaters of Crooked Creek locate the boy, who has survived on berries and slept in the hollow of an old stump. In a dramatic closing scene, a local minister informs the almost incredulous mother, whose faith in God has been severely tested, that her child has been found.

Updegraff closes by asserting that the searchers were rewarded "with the consciousness of having done their whole duty"—and that duty, of course, was to their fellow human beings, the people around them who formed the community of McDonough County pioneers. And she suggests that something precious is slipping away, for now there are "few left to tell us of pioneer life, in times long gone by."

It is hard to know for sure how much impact her remarkable account had, but several years later S.J. Clarke included a shortened version of "The Lost Child" in his *History of McDonough County*, remarking at the time that the serialized newspaper narrative had been "read with the greatest interest." The public response to it—as perhaps the best-loved local story—may have provided the inspiration for Clarke's noted chronicle of pioneer times, which he started planning later that year.

In October 1874, Updegraff married Joseph Gates, whom she had met at Lombard College, and moved to Oswego, Kansas, where she taught music, wrote for local newspapers, and was an energetic civic leader known for her independent views and social concern. She eventually died in 1930 at age eighty-one.

As the generations went by, there were other talented female rememberers who have also been forgotten. One was Henrietta (Martin) Campbell, who was the sister-in-law of S.J. Clarke. Unfortunately, her life was marked by tragedy. In 1884, she married Thomas B. Campbell, who was a local deputy sheriff, and they had but one child, who died as an infant. Years later, on March 31, 1903, her husband was stabbed to death by a prisoner whom he was transporting to the asylum at Jacksonville. Henrietta was devastated, but she then started a career in education, eventually serving as the Third Ward School principal for over twenty years.

She was a talented speaker and writer—and not just about education. To mark McDonough County's centennial in 1926, she gave a talk on "Social Life in the Early Settlement of Central Illinois," which was a superb account of both the domestic life of women—which she based on her own experience and that of her mother—and the importance of music in the lives of many pioneers. She provides the only local record of the many popular "singing games," in which "all the guests took part, singing in chorus and acting out the thought expressed in the songs as they marched or tripped along." Three old games especially liked by the pioneers were "Old Dan Tucker," "Skip to My Lou," and "Weavily Wheat," which she sang or chanted for the audience. She was then seventy years old.

Another outstanding voice of domestic life was Lora Lemmer, who came along much later. She was born in 1894 to a Macomb-area couple, Walter and Maggie Lemmer, who lived a few miles west of town. A shy woman, her life was almost completely enveloped by family relationships, and she never married, so her written recollections—most of them never published—focus on "Our Home," "Christmas Doings," "A Summer Sunday at Grandmother's," and similar topics. When I met Lora almost thirty years ago, I was astounded by the quality of her recall from very early years. I used to visit her at Everly House, where I taped her recollections of Macomb festivals, businesses, parks, and family life. I also printed her well-written memoir, "Decoration Day in 1900," in *Macomb: A Pictorial History*. She was my oldest friend. When she finally died at age ninety-nine, she had resided at Everly House for forty years.

Macomb's women may not have authored county histories over the years, but some of them—ever since Imogene Updegraff invaded the public forum with her stirring account of "The Lost Child"—have left historical works and recollections that have become increasingly precious as the years pass. And those talented writers have been especially insightful reflectors of family and community life.

W.H. Hainline and a Culture of Memory

Perhaps the most influential figure in Macomb and McDonough County during the decades following the Civil War was W.H. Hainline, the longtime editor of the *Macomb Journal*. He left more writing about the county's history, and about his own experience, than any other figure of his time, although it is scattered through more than five decades of newspaper issues. Those articles reveal a man of intense loyalty to the American cause and deep commitment to local culture—a culture that became, through his dedicated effort, remarkably devoted to remembering. His impact on the historical enterprise in McDonough County, including my own work generations later, would be immeasurable.

His parents, John and Margaret Hainline, came from Fayette County, Kentucky, during 1838 and bought a log cabin farmstead in Section 6 of Emmet Township, which later became known as the Spring Creek neighborhood. Over the years they raised eleven children. W.H. (William Henry) was born in 1841. As a boy, he acquired the nickname "Doc," simply because someone felt he looked or acted like a doctor.

As a 1907 biographical sketch states, he "was reared to farm work, and in the winters of his boyhood attended the common school in his neighborhood, where he wrestled with McGuffey's *Readers*, the elementary 'blue back' spelling book, Kirkham's *Grammar*, and Pike's and Ray's arithmetics." The Timber School, built in the 1840s, had "walls of rounded logs, a clapboard roof, a puncheon floor, slab seats, greased cloths for window lights, and a log fireplace," but however primitive the building, his studies there provided

An 1890s photograph of *Macomb Journal* editor W.H. Hainline.

Hainline with the foundation for a superb career in small-town journalism.

During the 1860 presidential campaign, he became an admirer of Lincoln and participated in local Republican rallies, so it is not surprising that, when the war came one year later, he immediately joined up. Hainline later did a vast amount of writing about his regiment and his own war experience, which is now being compiled and examined for a detailed historical overview of his achievements, but the essence of it is that he served from May 24, 1861, until July 8, 1865, as a private in Company A of the Sixteenth Illinois Infantry Regiment, composed largely of McDonough County men.

During those four years, his regiment skirmished in Missouri, fought in the Chattanooga campaign, and joined in Sherman's famous march through Georgia. On July 20, 1864, Hainline was captured at the Battle of Peach Tree Creek, near Atlanta, and was sent to Andersonville. For seventy days he endured the horrors of that legendary prison camp, where unsheltered and starving soldiers died every day. It was a devastating experience with a deep impact on his inner life.

Fortunately, he was exchanged with two thousand other Union prisoners, and after a period of recovery he rejoined his regiment, marching with Sherman's army through its devastating campaign to the sea. During that time, he participated in the capture of Atlanta, and then he marched with the Sixteenth up through the Carolinas. At the final battle of the campaign, at Bentonville, his beloved brother George, who commanded Company A, was killed when a cannonball tore his arm off while he was carrying the American flag.

After the war, the twenty-four-year-old Hainline was elected county treasurer in 1865, so he moved to Macomb, where he soon married. In 1867, he bought a drugstore and ran it for two years. His dispensing of medicine and kindly interest in the health of others gave new meaning to his nickname, "Doc."

In 1870, he sold the drugstore and bought a half interest in the *Macomb Journal*. The longtime editor, B.R. Hampton, had been elected a state senator, so he had to be in Springfield much of the time. Hampton sent in articles that were political reports and also started writing political and social satire under the pseudonym "Pawl Pry," but Hainline covered local matters, writing the "Personal" column, the "Our Chatter Box" commentary column, and an occasional "Town Saunterer's Diary," as well as many other articles. In his writings, the community and surrounding county became a vibrantly realized place. He also promoted blacks as members of the Macomb community and championed a wide range of public issues, from better schools to concern for the poor. He eventually bought out Hampton in 1881.

Although successful and popular, Hainline suffered a tragic loss. In 1874, his twenty-nine-year-old wife died, leaving him with two small daughters. Heartbroken, he wrote a touching obituary about her final days and his own sad situation, with "all plans for the future, all present happiness…destroyed." But five years later, he married Katherine Vorhees, and they had two more children. The younger one was Andrew L., known as Les, who idolized his kindly father and would later become a community leader, too.

Hainline never got over his Civil War experience. As the years passed, he wrote hundreds of articles relating to the war, including a sizable overview of "McDonough's Soldiers," histories of units, articles related to noted leaders, personal reminiscences, interviews with other soldiers, reprinted war letters, regimental reunion items, obituaries of countless "comrades," lists of veterans buried in county cemeteries, and Decoration Day pieces. He was obsessed with remembering and honoring local war veterans.

So Macomb became a town with perpetual remembrance of the war, and with a Memorial Day observance that was extensive and deeply meaningful—for surviving veterans, for families who had lost loved ones, and for younger residents who acknowledged and celebrated the slowly dwindling cadre of local heroes. No leader did more planning for those huge annual rituals than Hainline.

The busy editor was, in fact, devoted to public service. He was a county supervisor, an alderman, the mayor, and the postmaster. He was the longtime secretary of the County Fair Association, the commander of the Macomb GAR (Civil War veterans) post, and a trustee of two Illinois normal schools (or teachers' colleges). In the turn-of-the-century movement to establish a normal school in Macomb, Hainline was a leading figure. And he was, of course, a perpetual Republican Party leader too.

Hainline's retrospective focus was not limited to the war. He also wrote countless articles about the past in McDonough County, including masterful obituaries that celebrated people who had made outstanding contributions

A turn-of-the-century Memorial Day photograph showing the old wooden Oakwood Cemetery entrance and people gathering on the hillside for the annual program.

to community life. Through his pen, local heritage became a broadly shared experience and remembering was promoted as a civic virtue. On December 17, 1903, he produced a special issue of the *Journal* that was devoted entirely to the county's history. Late in his career, on July 28, 1922, he paid tribute to his forebears at the *Journal*, including B.R. Hampton, James K. Magie, and others, "who made it a power for good in the community." By then, Hainline had been known affectionately for years as "the Old Man of the *Journal*," a title that he enjoyed because it linked him to the long tradition of the newspaper that he loved.

When Hainline died on April 8, 1924, at the age of eighty-two, his passing was a kind of public event. Everyone knew that a significant moment in the town's history had occurred, that Macomb would never quite be the same again. The stores were closed during his funeral, which was attended by a huge crowd, including the last surviving members of the GAR. The minister who conducted the service simply read extracts from some of Hainline's newspaper articles, and "all who listened were deeply moved." Then a quartet sang his favorite song, "The Old Brigade." At Oakwood Cemetery, where he had participated in so many Decoration Day ceremonies, military riflemen fired a last salute, a bugler played "Taps," and then "mounds of flowers" from grateful townspeople were piled upon his grave.

Hainline's obituary in the *Macomb Journal* ran for seven columns, and it was soon followed by tributes from other newspaper editors in the county and the region. As the editor of the *Blandinsville Star Gazette* put it, he "was a wise, able, kindly soul, of keen intelligence and broad sympathies," and he had a greater influence on local people "than any other man who ever lived in the county." He was clearly a kind of spiritual leader—not in matters of faith, but in sensitive regard for others and service to the community.

Even in the twenty-first century, it is hard to examine Hainline's well-focused, purpose-driven life or read his immense body of newspaper writings, so often devoted to appreciating others, without being continually impressed by his character and increasingly committed to the town that he loved.

C.V. Chandler: Macomb as a Meaningful Place

Rarely in the history of a town does a man come along whose unparalleled talent for business leadership is matched by his devotion to the community. More than a century ago, Macomb's C.V. Chandler so effectively combined those qualities for so long that his impact on the town was immeasurable. And as with W.H. Hainline, his deep sense of belonging became fused with his Civil War memories and relationships.

Chandler was born in the pioneer village of Macomb on January 25, 1843. During his earliest years, his family lived on the corner of Lafayette and Adams Streets, but in 1850 they moved closer to the square. Many years later, he recalled the appearance of the town at that time: "Every business house was on the public square, and then the square was not filled with business houses. The old Bartleson home stood on the southeast corner of the square, occupying three lots. Our home, after my father moved from north of the railroad, was at the present site of the *Journal*. Our garden was where the Illinois Theatre now stands."

His father, Charles Chandler, was a well-to-do land dealer (Macomb's first real estate agent) and, later, the owner of a bank. Hence, after his mother died in 1855, C.V. attended private schools at Danbury, Connecticut, and Lake Forest, Illinois. Perhaps because he was sent away for long periods, the youth came to love his hometown like few people who have ever lived in it.

As a teenager, C.V. met Abraham Lincoln during his October 1858 speaking visit to Macomb, for the senatorial candidate was a dinner guest at the Chandler home, and the young Republican enthusiast drove him around

A reunion of Civil War veterans, with C.V. Chandler standing at the left. Photograph taken at the turn of the century.

town in the family carriage. Later, in 1860, the bright, talented youngster was a page at the Republican Convention in Chicago, where Lincoln was nominated for president.

The Civil War also had a lasting influence on C.V. In 1862, as he was preparing to enter Williams College, he suddenly returned to Macomb and enlisted as a private in Company I of the Seventy-eighth Illinois Infantry, which had many officers and men from Macomb. Nine months later, after serving with the regiment in Kentucky and Tennessee, he was promoted to second lieutenant.

On September 20, 1863, he was wounded in both thighs at the Battle of Chickamauga. Because there was no medical attention, he resorted to removing the rifle ball from his leg with a penknife. Chandler was sent home to recover, and by the time he returned to his regiment, he had been promoted to adjutant. However, his old wound soon forced him to resign his commission.

Upon returning to Macomb, he embarked on a remarkable business career. While serving as a teller in his father's bank, he built and bought buildings until he owned eight brick structures on the square—not to mention the opera house block (known as "Chandler's Block"), which he constructed in 1873 on the site of his former home. For half a century, that lovely auditorium was the venue for numerous plays, musicals, lectures, minstrel shows, and local ceremonies. It symbolized Macomb's cultural attainment as it also promoted a sense of community. The dedication ceremony on April 21, 1873, featured a patriotic drama, *Child of the Regiment*, which fostered recollections of the war.

A second "Chandler's Block" was constructed across the street, on what is now an empty lot, and the Chandler (later Pace) Hotel went up soon afterward a block or so north of the opera house.

When his father died in 1878, C.V. became president of the First National Bank. He was later president of the Bank of Bardolph and the People's State Bank of Colchester as well. But those institutions were only part of his business empire. He was also a founder of the first Macomb pottery, president of the Macomb Wagon Company, treasurer of the Macomb Calendar Clock Company, a director of the Macomb Tile and Sewer Pipe Company, and a major investor in several other local businesses. Noted for his encouragement of new enterprises, he was a one-man chamber of commerce.

Fortunately, Chandler was also dedicated to serving the community in other ways. He was city treasurer during the 1870s and 1880s, an alderman from 1893 to 1899, and treasurer of the Western Illinois Normal School Board of Trustees early in the twentieth century. He was also a member of various civic groups and, very much like his friend W.H. Hainline, was a leading figure in the McDonough County GAR. Every year during the Memorial Day observance at Oakwood Cemetery, he would read the list of local veterans who had died during and since the war. Of course, the list slowly got longer and longer, but for him, such remembrance was a sacred obligation—like a religious ritual. At the turn of the century, he also served the state as president of the Illinois Soldiers' Home Board of Trustees. That facility was, and is still, located in Quincy.

Chandler also found time for an active family life. He married Clara Baker on August 28, 1866, and they eventually had six children. The Chandlers lived at the corner of Carroll and McArthur Streets.

His greatest single service to the community came when he bought up the buildings on the city block north of the square, removed them, planted trees, and gave the land to Macomb as a park. Acquiring the land took years because the block contained two churches, two lumberyards, a planning mill, a carpenter's shop, a gas service building, and two residences. Opened for community use in 1879, it was finally deeded to the city in 1893. Since then, it has become an indispensable place to gather, celebrate, and remember.

In 1899, Chandler also donated the memorial to McDonough County Civil War soldiers that still stands on the west side of the park. It cost $4,000—a huge sum at that time—and was dedicated with an elaborate ceremony that included a parade. The statue on top depicts an infantry soldier standing at ease, as if he had accomplished his mission, and carved on the front of the pedestal is the image of a GAR badge. For the local public, it prompted communal remembrance of their huge commitment and sacrifice.

Shortly after the turn of the century, Chandler embarked on his most ambitious project, the establishment of the Macomb and Western Illinois Railroad. It was designed to carry passengers to and from Industry and Littleton, to provide nearby farmers with a means of shipping grain and livestock to market, and eventually to connect the town with other important railroads.

The venture was not only expensive but also difficult, and when money tightened up, many of those whom Chandler had once helped refused to support the project. In 1910, the incredible occurred: Chandler went bankrupt. He not only lost the railroad but all of his property and business interests as well, even the bank that had been started by his father before the Civil War. The sixty-seven-year-old man was crushed. He packed his bags and left Macomb to live with his son in Indianapolis.

But he was not consumed by bitterness, preferring instead to remember the many wonderful experiences that marked his years in Macomb. As he became elderly, he was especially sad at having to miss the annual Memorial Day programs, and so each year on May 30 he got out his gold McDonough County GAR badge (a gift from his comrades when he erected the statue)

The monument to McDonough County's Civil War soldiers, given to Macomb by C.V. Chandler, was dedicated in 1899.

and wore it at his new location. A 1922 recollective letter, sent to W.H. Hainline, reflects the meaning of Memorial Day for Chandler, which was so obviously bound up, through experiences and relationships, with his deep sense of belonging to Macomb:

> *Dear Doc:*
>
> *...I notice that you are giving the Memorial Day program its usual prominence, for which accept my thanks. It remains for rural communities, small towns, and cities "to not forget" and hold the day sacred....*
>
> *I well remember the first one we observed, in the 60's, when the living comrades were detailed in squads for each* [dead] *comrade's grave. Now the great majority are "over there."....*
>
> *On the first Memorial Day, I took in my carriage to the old cemetery, west of town, down on the old Campbell land, hub deep in mud, Capt. G.L. Farwell, Dr. W.F. Bayne, and Dr. J.B. Kyle—now all gone to their reward....*
>
> *Doc, I don't want to be the last GAR man, but would like to stay a little longer, and when I come to make my last visit to Macomb, I hope you and*

enough comrades who know me will be there to lay me away, with the flag we loved so well, under the green sod that comes each spring, beneath the waving, sighing trees of beautiful "Oakwood."

Yours in F.C. and L. [Fraternity, Charity, and Loyalty, the motto of the GAR],

Comrade C.V. Chandler

As the years went by, more and more people in Macomb began to recognize the enormous debt that was owed to the little old man who had led the community unselfishly for forty years. A movement was started to gather donations for a C.V. Chandler Memorial, and it included leaders associated with every notable organization in town, from the City Council and GAR to the Rotary Club and Women's Club. A huge brick arch was eventually erected in the park that he had given to the community.

Finally, on September 17, 1929, Chandler was invited back to Macomb for the dedication of the arch. People came by the hundreds to shake his hand, express their thanks for the park, and wish him well. At a ceremony that afternoon, the elderly white-haired man was introduced to the crowd, and their applause thundered from every corner of Chandler Park. The people of Macomb had finally proven themselves worthy of the gift. In a sense, it was the town's finest moment.

When C.V. Chandler died, on October 20, 1934, Macomb lost its greatest booster and most devoted citizen. He was a man who recognized that wealth and influence bring enormous obligations to act for the public good and who deeply understood that community membership is more than a matter of location. It is a commitment to the place that has made your own life meaningful.

Alexander McLean: Leader and Historian

The most noted immigrant in early McDonough County was Alexander McLean, who came as a teenager from Scotland. A bright, talented, uncommonly literate man, he became the finest mayor of Macomb in the nineteenth century. He also led many organizations and produced a notable county history.

Born in Glasgow on September 24, 1833, McLean came to America and McDonough County with his parents in 1849. They temporarily settled at Camp Creek and then moved to Macomb in 1850. As a youngster, McLean cut and hauled stone for his father, who owned a quarry west of town. But he was an avid reader who "devoured volume upon volume of books," on many subjects—including politics and theology, as a biographical sketch later pointed out. Like Lincoln, he was determined to rise.

His big break came in about 1853, when he was hired by circuit clerk William H. Randolph to serve as his deputy, or assistant. McLean's broad knowledge, speaking and writing skills, charming manners, and solid work ethic soon made him a successful and popular public official. That job led to an acquaintance with many families, and he later married Martha Randolph, the daughter of a merchant on the square, at the close of 1856. They eventually had ten children.

McLean also worked with William H. Randolph in a real estate firm, which led to a job in New York as the clerk of a real estate company, from 1864 to 1871. For whatever reasons, he did not serve in the Civil War. After moving back to Macomb, he opened the McDonough County Real Estate Agency, which became the most successful real estate business of that era.

He was soon elected mayor. In four consecutive one-year terms (1873–77), he proved himself the finest mayor of the century. As *Macomb Journal* editor W.H. Hainline later said, "In the four years that he held the office of Mayor, more public improvements were made than during any similar period in the history of the city; more sidewalks were built and kept in good repair, more miles of road faithfully worked; a handsome and costly schoolhouse erected and paid for; gas was introduced, and many other things were accomplished." All of that was achieved during the worst depression America had yet experienced.

After leaving office, McLean continued his leadership. He was one of the original trustees of the public library, in 1881, and was later president of the Macomb Board of Education. On a state level, he served on the University of Illinois Board of Trustees for thirty years. Those three roles suggest his uncommon commitment to self-growth through learning. Extremely popular, he was also a leader in various fraternal and benevolent groups, including the Masons, Odd Fellows, Knights of Pythias, United Workmen, and Independent Order of Mutual Aid. In most of them he held state offices.

A very committed Christian, as well as a supporter of education, he was the most well-known figure in the huge McDonough County Sunday School Association, and for many years he edited the "Sunday School" column in the *Macomb Journal*, promoting Bible studies and reporting on Christian educational efforts. Moreover, in the spring of 1874, when he was a first-term mayor, there was a huge "union" religious revival, the greatest of the century, which went on for weeks, with "The Opera House Crowded Nightly—and Street Meetings Through the Days," as the *Journal* headline put it. McLean was a longtime proponent of such interdenominational cooperation, so his election as mayor had surely inspired the effort.

Early in the twentieth century, he decided to write a more up-to-date history of McDonough County. S.J. Clarke's had appeared in 1878, and an even longer, anonymous one had appeared in 1885. But McLean wanted to appreciate some more recent community leaders who had contributed to the business and cultural development of the town and county. And he was interested in what drove successful people—"the motive power that lies out of sight," that works "behind and beneath the activities of outward life," and that "forms citizens" and "shapes the course of communities," as his county history indicates. For that reason, half of his 450-page, oversized book is devoted to biographical sketches—some 470 of them. His broad acquaintance with pioneers is revealed by his detailed accounts of figures

The real estate and fraternal organization office of Alexander McLean at the turn of the century. McLean is standing second from the right.

like John Harris, who had come in the late 1820s and could vividly recall the struggle to survive in an undeveloped wilderness; Jonathan H. Baker, who had clerked for James M. Campbell in the 1830s and later became a county judge; and Charles Blandin, whose father had laid out Blandinsville in the 1840s.

One original section that comes early in the book is a chapter on native animals. McLean provides, for example, a vivid account of the wolf hunts that were common in the county during the pre–Civil War years, and he discusses the "numerous and deadly" rattlesnakes that were also present on the frontier. In fact, he recalls a time when he was plowing in a wheat field and his horse was bitten and died, leaving him with "a great dread of rattlesnakes." In contrast, he mentions delightful memories of bird life, including the immense flocks of passenger pigeons, "which literally darkened the sky, passing along like the sound of a mighty wind," and the noisy flocks of sandhill cranes, which "joined in a sort of pow-wow, leaping, dancing, and screaming wildly" whenever they were disturbed. He matches that chapter with a helpful one on the county's native flora. He was clearly impacted by his personal experience with the natural world.

The book also includes an interesting section on "Old Settlers" that documents the development of a very recent social group, "the Pioneer Club of McDonough County, organized in August, 1905, and now containing a membership of nearly three hundred, whose ages range from seventy to 101 years." McLean himself, who was seventy-two then, was perhaps the leading organizer, and surely one of his purposes was to develop greater acquaintance with older residents of the county, whose memories could be helpful for the writing of a new county history. Deeply rooted, they would also be his most interested readers. The group was actually derived from the Macomb Old Men's Club, an informal organization that had been around for years. The Pioneer Club, which included women, reflected the generational pride of older people in the county, who had witnessed so much cultural change and were rapidly disappearing.

McLean knew that he would soon vanish also. Shortly after starting his book, he contracted colon cancer. But true to his task-oriented nature, he pushed on with the project, completing the huge book within two years. Just a few weeks after it appeared, in the early fall of 1907, he died.

His funeral was held at the Baptist church, where he had been a leader for so long. According to the *Macomb Journal*, "The building was packed to standing room" as the townspeople turned out to honor a man who had been both "a history-maker" and "a history writer"—who had helped to shape the progress of his county and then had struggled to preserve its eighty-year heritage.

James Burns and the Culture of History

Among the teachers who came to Macomb with the establishment of Western Illinois State Normal School, none had a greater impact on the community than James Burns. The school's first history professor—and later a Latin teacher—he was also the town's first public intellectual, a well-educated man who spoke to, and for, the people of his locality.

Born in 1850, and raised on a farm near Graysville in western Pennsylvania, young James studied for a year in the preparatory department of Waynesburg College, in his home county, right after the Civil War. Then he taught in rural schools for a few years before coming to Illinois in 1869 to attend Monmouth College, where he also taught Latin before he even graduated. The brilliant young man received an AB degree there in 1875.

Burns married a classmate, Ida Carey, and was a principal and superintendent in four small towns before returning to Monmouth as superintendent of schools in 1888. He held that post for thirteen years and then headed the school system in nearby Aledo for one year before the opportunity arose to teach at the new normal (or teacher training) school in Macomb.

Because he had been a longtime superintendent in the western Illinois region, Burns knew many area teachers, and perhaps for that reason, President John W. Henninger asked him to recruit and register students. He was, then, Western's first registrar, in 1902, as well as the initial faculty member in history.

It was surely the opportunity to teach history, and to prepare others for teaching it, if only on an elementary-school level, that drew Burns to the

Early Western historian and Latin teacher James C. Burns. Photograph taken at about the time WISNS opened, 1902.

new position. He not only loved that field—especially American history and Illinois history, which would be his main concerns—but he was also a born crusader, both for education and for the insights that historical understanding can engender in the public mind.

Among his surviving papers are not only professional and classroom lectures on "History: Its Method and Function in a Normal School," "The History of Illinois," and related matters, but also talks with a broader focus. In an address called "Moral and Humane Education," early in the century, he lamented, "We are educating the head but not the heart. [We teach] knowing, thinking, reasoning, judging, and discriminating. But reverence, sympathy, tenderness, patience, love, and kindness are neglected." Of course, he felt that an awareness of history was part of the answer. In a remarkable 1906 lecture called "The Culture of History," he addresses the very impact of historical comprehension on the human mind and heart, viewing it as an essential, shaping, cultural force: "In history we hear the very heartbeat of the race, as it struggles with temptation or rises on the wings of aspiration. It reveals our duty to ourselves, and to our neighbors."

As that quotation reveals, Burns was an eloquent and powerful speaker who rapidly developed a reputation not only among the would-be teachers at Western but among the Macomb-area public as well. In 1904, for example, he gave a riveting Memorial Day address, the likes of which local people had never heard before. Determined to reveal the tragic impact of the Civil War, he said,

> *Conceive of a cyclone of terrific force, sweeping over McDonough County, killing or maiming every man, woman, and child in the county, and yet the loss of life would fall 10,000 short of the loss in the Battle of Chickamauga.... And 6,000 more men fell at Gettysburg than the combined voting populations of Rock Island, Mercer, Warren, Henderson, McDonough, and Hancock counties....*

> *What part did McDonough County play in this great drama?... With a population of 20,000, in 1860, the county sent 3,000 men, or one seventh of the entire population, into the field.*

He went on to give an overview of the roles played by several regiments that had recruits from McDonough County; he praised the local soldiers, living and dead, for their "heroic achievement," and he called upon his listeners to preserve American liberty. His very stirring address was printed in the *Macomb Journal*.

Burns was also revered as a teacher. As one article about him commented, "He seemed to act in a sort of position as father confessor to the students, and they went to him with their troubles...whether in his class or in others, and they were always kindly received, and the help tendered whenever possible." He and his wife also brought in, from the war-ravaged Philippines, the first foreign students, who resided at the new Burns home on West Adams Street (later the Brooks Cultural Center).

No wonder students and local residents were shocked when the second Western president, Alfred Bayliss, fired Burns, along with several other teachers, in 1906, because they did not have graduate degrees.

Burns became the superintendent of schools in Vandalia, a historic Illinois town, but was almost immediately hired to come back, in 1907, as the superintendent of schools in Macomb. In that position, he continued his work as a public intellectual, speaking on Abraham Lincoln and spearheading the local Lincoln centennial celebration in 1909; delivering another stirring Memorial Day address in 1910; and lecturing on American and Illinois history to local groups. An ardent Christian, he also led a Bible study class for twenty years that had some seventy-five men enrolled.

Re-hired at Western by President Walter P. Morgan, in 1913, to teach Latin, Burns—then sixty-three years old—continued his crusade for public awareness of history. He organized "The Military Tract Celebration of the 100th Anniversary of the Battle of Plattsburgh," which featured the dedication of the monument to General Alexander Macomb and Commodore Thomas Macdonough, in Chandler Park, on September 11, 1914. And he spoke on that occasion, along with Senator L.Y. Sherman.

He also spearheaded the formation of the McDonough County Historical Society, calling an initial meeting on November 30, 1920. The only professional historian in the group, he did not assume control, realizing that the organization's success depended on generating local leadership from among those who were deeply rooted in the county. But he continued to publicize and promote it.

In 1926, Burns was a leading figure in the McDonough County Centennial Celebration, lecturing on county participation in early military conflicts, starting with the Black Hawk War, and he also spoke on "America's Sesquicentennial," which was celebrated in that same year. He and his wife even created an exhibit of antiques—dishes, quilts, and other items—in a downtown store window for the local centennial.

The aging historian continued to teach at Western, and during the 1920s he was affectionately known as "Daddy Burns." One of his last publications was a 1927 article on prominent Western alumni, written for the school's twenty-fifth anniversary. By then, he was the last of the original Western faculty members who still taught. When he finally retired in the spring of 1930, he was seventy-eight, and he had been teaching for an incredible period of time, sixty-four years. A few months later, he died.

Of the hundreds of Western faculty whose lives I have looked into, and whose values, struggles, and accomplishments I have tried to appreciate, none has been more personally inspiring. Burns had the right idea: his focus was not only on helping his students but on serving the people of his locale as well. For him, history was more than a career; it was a calling, an expression of his spiritual life. His example and his words continue to have an impact.

Alex Holmes and the Personal Past

Very much like C.V. Chandler, Macomb resident Alex Holmes had a profound sense of place. He did not start writing for the newspaper until 1914, when he was sixty-nine, but he continued through World War I and the 1920s, both helping countless others relate to the local past and reflecting upon his own experience. To him, the past that mattered was always personal, and he wrote for the townspeople whom he cared about.

He was born in Farmington on January 6, 1845, and spent his earliest years there and in nearby western Peoria County. When his family moved to Macomb, two years before the railroad arrived, he was just eight years old. Decades later, he depicted their arrival and their impoverished circumstances:

> *Father, mother, four boys, and four girls came to Macomb from Peoria County, in October 1853, and moved into a two-room house with a lean-to summer kitchen, belonging to James M. Campbell, located on West Carroll Street…. My brother Willie was born there in 1855. We lived in that house until April 1857, when Father built about the same-sized house* [sixteen by twenty-two feet] *at 1020 East Washington Street. On June 12 sister Ida was born there. Father was sick from June 1858 until February 1859; he did no work in all that time….*
>
> *Father, mother, and ten children. It took nearly all the room space to set up beds, and each one had a trundle bed under it…. The summer kitchen was our bath room, when it was warm enough to use it, or when it was*

> *absolutely necessary to take a bath. We had just enough* [food] *to keep from going hungry.*

Raised in Ohio, his father, Willis Holmes, was a talented but impractical carpenter. He invented a windmill in 1860, which he hoped would lift the family out of poverty, but it was ineffective and did not sell. He lost money, and the family lost their tiny house. They returned to renting, first on East Jackson Street, then on East Carroll Street, and then on East Calhoun Street—three places in three years. And during that time—the awful Civil War era, marked by local conflict, military deaths, and economic depression—another brother and a sister also died, and two more children were born.

So, the story of Alex Holmes's childhood is like something from a Dickens novel, and that's what makes it so special. His parents were not educated; they were not owners or people with well-established relatives who might help. They were strugglers, experiencing privation and death. Willis Holmes finally built another small house, on South Campbell Street, in 1864. By then, nineteen-year-old Alex, long done with his limited schooling, had been working with his father to help support the family since he was twelve. But to his credit, he was never bitter. "I was one of twelve children," he said. "I have no complaint to make."

Macomb businessman and revered local historian Alex Holmes.

Sixty years later, as a local historian, he repeatedly recalled the family's arrival and struggle, as if that were the crucial, destiny-making time of his life. And it was. Part of the reason was that, as he later said, "I had never seen a town [he could not recall Farmington]," and "I wanted to know all [about Macomb] that was to be known." While the family's experience was hard, their likeable, easygoing son Alex rapidly made friends, with adults as well as other youngsters, and as he later put it, "within a short time I knew 90 percent of the people in Macomb."

In a sense, the community became his extended family, and as he eventually realized, the people and places of that era "became indelibly fixed in my memory." Many of his later "Reminiscence" pieces include detailed accounts of the dense network of family relationships in mid-nineteenth-century Macomb.

Holmes also started keeping a diary in 1867, the year he married Martha Sosman, and those volumes later prompted a host of recollections. Among the many aspects of the town that he recounted in his frequent writings for the *Journal* were Chandler Park (1914), McDonough College (1921), the Old Macomb Cemetery (1921), the Methodist church (1922, 1923), Campbell's Hall (1924), Chandler's Opera House (1925), the Catholic church (1925), the early mills (1924), the early hotels (1925), and the coming of the railroad (1926)—not to mention a dozen accounts of residential streets and businesses around the square.

His articles often ramble, revealing that he experienced the past as all people did centuries ago—not as a linear progression of temporal units (days, years, decades), bringing cultural change, but as a network of interconnected images and narratives. His recollections remind us that the past is, for everyone, a psychological reality—and his writings are commonly filled with long-gone people and places. Who besides him has recalled the family of town founder James M. Campbell, the widow of Civil War hero William Broaddus, the apple orchard on Townsend Hill—which later became Oakwood Cemetery—or the woods called Liberty Grove, a few blocks south of the square, where the early townspeople held their Fourth of July picnics?

His comments on people are generally brief, but they are all we have about some early residents. One of my favorites is his poignant account of circus acrobat Wilson Wolf:

> *Wilse Wolf, son of Joe Wolf, a cabinet maker who for many years worked for* [undertaker] *B.F. Martin, went out* [into the circus world] *as a high tumbler and was among the champions of the world in his line. He could leave the springboard and turn* [somersaults] *three times in the air over 13 horses standing side by side…. He was a near neighbor of mine, and I saw him during his last sickness…. Wilse Wolf, after traveling for a time, was here with the Burr Robbins circus. The show was held on the site where Godowski's coal yard is now. He there made one of his high leaps, turning three times over 13 horses. Shortly after this he hurt himself in one of his leaps* [in 1874, at Chicago], *took tuberculosis of the bowels,*

> *came home, and died, on West Jefferson Street. The undertakers did not undertake as much as they do now, so I helped to lay him out. He was simply skin and bones. His knees looked like cantaloupes with broom sticks run through them. His knees were enlarged, I suppose, from the shocks in his tumbling.*

Wilson Wolf died on July 15, 1875, at the age of twenty-four. This is part of a 1920 reminiscence about the James T. Johnson circus, which was organized in Macomb after the Civil War and then toured the country. Holmes points out that a number of local men were performers or workers in that circus.

As that account reveals, his writing was often the most engaging when it was autobiographical, focused on people he interacted with or things that he did or witnessed. One item, "The Occupations of My Life" (1923), recounts his work experience, from childhood jobs like "grinding tan bark" at the Walker tannery and "peddling apples and peaches around the square and down at the old depot," when he was ten, to later work as a carpenter, apple shipper, cider maker, junk collector, second-hand store owner, mill operator, business investor, and, finally, real estate developer. Concerning the last of those, he said, "I made good [money] at that business," and indeed he did. There are three Holmes Additions to Macomb, which he laid out to sell lots. He also constructed the Holmes Building (now the children's section of Macomb Public Library) in 1925. The poor boy who had fallen in love with Macomb eventually achieved real success.

A few of his most poignant articles are really personal essays. One, titled "Meditation in Oakwood Cemetery" (1918), provides an engaging illustration of memory in the life of an older person:

> *While attending Decoration Day services last week, I tarried in our beautiful cemetery, and my memory ran back 63 years to the time I was a light-hearted boy eating apples from the trees that grew on the ground located near where I was sitting….*
>
> *The first burials there were 61 years ago. My brother James was buried in September 1858. There were very few graves here at that time. A Mr. Moore was the first one buried in the new cemetery, near the west side…. Now there are between 3,700 and 4,000 graves. The Silent City has about kept pace with the growth of our city. Our fathers, mothers, brothers, sisters, wives, husbands, children, playmates, schoolmates, teachers, soldiers, and citizens generally, are lying all around us.*

The Holmes building, built in 1925, later became the children's section of the Macomb Public Library. Alex is standing in front of it.

As this reveals, Holmes knew that he was not just speaking to his fellow townspeople but for them, reflecting the community's consciousness of dead relatives and friends.

His sense of connection with the dead at Oakwood Cemetery was partly influenced by his persistent recording of local deaths in his diary—as if he were determined to let no one escape the bounds of his memory—and partly by his service to local families as a pallbearer, as he said late in his life:

> *I have kept a diary 62 years up to last January. I have noted the deaths of people in Macomb from children to old age* [folks]*.... I have acted as pallbearer for a young child and for an old lady 101 years old. It is frequently hard to get pallbearers among busy men. I was busy, but never too busy to act in this capacity when asked.... I do not think it an exaggeration to say, I have acted* [as pallbearer] *at least 250 times.*

Interestingly, his earliest article for the *Journal*, on April 14, 1914, recalls his role as a pallbearer for two neighbors, a small boy and the child's grandmother, who died in early April 1876, and whose bodies had to be carried by hand through deep mud to Oakwood. As such efforts suggest, he had a remarkable sense of commitment to others in the community. In another personal essay on Oakwood Cemetery, which starts with a friend's funeral, he also reflects on the social consequences of old age: "I have known more of those in the Silent City than I now know among the living in Macomb at this time. If I do not make friends with the young, I shall soon be left without a friend, for nearly all of them my age have passed on."

Actually, he still had a number of friends and an even larger number of admirers among those who read his articles in the *Journal*, or who later owned a copy of his collection, *The History and Reminiscences of Alex Holmes*, which appeared in 1924, printed by his son, Dr. J.B. Holmes. When he finally died in 1931, at age eighty-six, his funeral service at the Methodist church drew a standing-room-only crowd, and his obituary referred to him, quite rightly, as "one of Macomb's oldest, best known, and best loved citizens." As that suggests, and his life reveals, you have to encounter, befriend, appreciate, and eventually remember others in order to belong. Alex Holmes showed everyone how it was done.

Quincy Hainline, the Old Storyteller

Along with Alex Holmes, the other well-known voice of the past during the 1920s was Quincy Hainline, a retired farmer who called himself "The Old Storyteller." The younger brother of *Macomb Journal* editor W.H. Hainline, he drew his most interesting material from the heritage of Spring Creek, a rural neighborhood northwest of Macomb where he lived for most of his long life, and he became the final spokesman for the pioneer experience in McDonough County.

Born in 1848 in an Emmet Township log cabin, he was seven years younger than his brother William H. ("Doc") Hainline, and that made a huge difference: He was just thirteen when the Civil War broke out, so he never served. His responsibility was to help his aging parents on the farm while his older brothers did the fighting—and demonstrated their manhood and their patriotism. He did not experience the life-changing horrors of war or the intense comradeship of the GAR veterans. In a sense, he lived in the shadow of his heroic brothers—George, who commanded Company A of the Sixteenth Regiment and was killed in one of the war's final battles, at Bentonville, and Doc, who served through the entire war and survived Andersonville.

Quincy Hainline's emergence as a noted rememberer of the county's past was prompted partly because his father, John D. Hainline, and grandfather, George, had come to the Spring Creek area in 1838, and John was a popular storyteller who himself became known as "the last of the pioneers of the Spring Creek Settlement" before his death in 1901. Quincy idolized his

Quincy Hainline and his second wife, Ella, in the 1890s.

father and was much like him. Also, his brother Doc's constant focus on the Civil War and tracking of Civil War veterans in the *Journal* led to a 1917 article by Quincy on soldiers from "the old Spring Creek neighborhood," and that in turn led to a 1919 article on pioneer farming, which appeared just after he had retired and rented out the old family farm.

Also, the new McDonough County Historical Society wanted to locate the trail through the county that had been taken by Lincoln's company of soldiers during the Black Hawk War. Because of his knowledge of the county's heritage northwest of Macomb, Hainline was asked to locate the northern half of that trail. In "The Lincoln Trail" (1920), he not only tracked the route of Lincoln's 1832 military company but also commented on various historic sites in the area, including the James Clarke log cabin (built in the 1830s), the Spring Creek Cemetery (started in 1834), and the Hainline log cabin, where he was born.

The praise he received for that investigation and report led to an invitation from the new historical society to write more generally about the Spring Creek settlement, so he produced a three-part series for the *Journal* called

"Pioneer Days." That series includes detailed accounts of building a log cabin and breaking the prairie soil—which he had learned about from his father's generation—and a striking section on Spring Creek's response to the Civil War. By the war era, he was a teenager, so his account of the homefront has the authority of personal experience. As he points out, the hub of that rural community was the post office:

> *My father, then postmaster, took two daily papers, the* Chicago Tribune *and the* Burlington Hawkeye. *The patrons of the office would come and wait anxiously for the arrival of the stage. We would also hear by telegraph of big battles, such as Shiloh, Corinth, Stone River, Lookout Mountain, Chickamauga…and dozens of others fought in the West, where we knew that the "settlement boys" were likely to be. So when the papers came…it was with hope and fear that we scanned the list* [of killed and wounded], *and many sad scenes the writer witnessed during those days.*

In that 1922 series, he recalled reading of the capture of his brother, Doc, and his cousin, James Hainline, near Atlanta, and later of the death of his oldest brother, George, at Bentonville.

Two years later, Quincy wrote a pair of articles focused on George's Civil War letters, which he had kept for sixty years. One of them depicts a late evening battle at Resaca, Georgia, and then his brother's response to the mass of dead bodies: "The word 'fire!' was given, and it seemed as if the heavens were lit up by the flash of musketry…and when [the enemy] fell back, 2,500 mangled and torn bodies lay on our front. They lay there the next morning, and what a sight…. As I looked on the cold, dead faces, I thought of the tears of father, mother, sister, wife, and sweetheart, and I cried in my heart, 'Oh, this cruel war.'"

After Doc died in 1924, Quincy wrote a tribute to him, which imaginatively reconstructs what must have been the most wrenching experience in his brother's entire life, the burial of George on the battlefield:

> *In a vision I see that brother* [Doc]*…as he places in a long trench, beside a hundred of his comrades,* [with] *his worn and faded blue uniform for a shroud, his knapsack for a pillow, and his ragged blanket for a winding sheet and coffin, that elder brother who had been his comrade and father through four years of blood and carnage,* [whom] *he must leave in a soldier's grave under the shadow of the North Carolina pines.*

He also mentions their shared grief at the close of the war: "Though almost three score years have passed, the writer can still see [Doc's] homecoming as if it were but yesterday—our tears of joy mixed with those of sorrow for the vacant chair."

Hainline also wrote a number of other Spring Creek memoirs, including an account of the family's log cabin homestead (built in 1838), a story of rowdyism at a Peter Cartwright camp meeting, and a two-part series on the 1860 Lincoln campaign.

Other local history articles went far beyond Spring Creek. My favorite is "The County's Worst Desperadoes," a two-part overview of the Maxwell brothers, published in 1924, which helped to spark the research that resulted in my *Dime Novel Desperadoes.* As it turns out, he had known them in the 1870s, when they lived on a rented farm north of Colchester. His account is often vague, not always accurate, and strikingly incomplete, but it must have been fascinating for his readers. It was for me.

Hainline had broad historical interests, so he also wrote articles unrelated to McDonough County, on the Mormons at Nauvoo, the Oregon Trail, the Spanish-American War, and other topics, but they were not as compelling as his more local items.

Like his brother Doc, Quincy Hainline had an enormous sense of responsibility to the Civil War dead, and that led to a few of his best articles, which were really personal essays. In a 1929 piece called "Marking Graves," he revealed that for decades each spring he had "made a yearly pilgrimage to the Walker and Spring Creek cemeteries," close to where he had always lived, and placed flags at the graves of dead soldiers. That spring, as he moved reverently from grave to grave, he reflected that he had known them all, and he shared a few memories, reminding his readers that the dead were not just names on headstones, but a presence in at least one person's mind. Then he finished at a family marker that mentioned his brother, "G.L. Hainline, 16th Ill.," whose body lay somewhere near Bentonville but who always got a flag, too.

Quincy was, to the last, the younger brother whose sacred mission was not to fight, not to die or endure, but to remember, and he continued to do that until old age slowly brought an end to his writing in the early 1930s. When he died on May 21, 1940, at age ninety-one, the last public rememberer who identified with the log cabin pioneers of McDonough County, and the final voice of the now vanished settlement of Spring Creek, was gone.

Bushnell Poet
Marian Stearns Curry

The most well-known recollective writings associated with Bushnell are poems written by a woman who grew up there early in the twentieth century and then lived in larger Illinois and Iowa towns. Because she did not reside in McDonough County during her long writing career, few local people know much about the author of *The Ballads of Bushnell.*

Marian Stearns Curry was born on December 27, 1896, probably at her grandparents' farm northwest of Walnut Grove. Those were her mother's parents, David and Sarah Crawford. He was a blacksmith who had come to Illinois in the 1850s, had eventually gone into farming, and had become very successful. Years later, in a memoir on the Crawfords, Curry depicted her grandfather as a religious man of "unassailable integrity" who was "a leader in church and community" for many years.

The poet's father, Paul Stearns, was a Prairie City farmer and also a talented musician. Her mother, Mary Crawford, also loved music and had a beautiful voice. She was a bright young woman who attended the Bushnell Conservatory of Music. Her teacher was Professor Edwin Wyckoff, who often led the town orchestra at the Bushnell Opera House. The young couple was married in 1891.

The Stearns family soon moved to Bushnell, where they lived in a sizable two-story home at 777 Rile Street. An only child, Marian always had lovely clothes, and her mother's social ambitions soon led to her daughter's first career, as a child model. Marian was, in fact, a lovely preschool girl with blonde curly hair, and her image soon appeared on calendars and sheet music.

Marian Stearns Curry in her late thirties, when she had just moved to Peoria. Photograph taken in 1935. *Courtesy of the Bushnell Historical Society.*

When she was a child, Bushnell had two carriage factories, two lumberyards, three banks, six blacksmith shops, three furniture stores, eight clothing and jewelry stores, eight restaurants, five groceries, four drug stores, several dry goods and hardware shops, two hotels, and an opera house.

Marian's parents wanted her to be a musician, and partly for that reason, her mother took her to many local cultural events—which provided memories that later inspired some of her Bushnell poems. But Marian found her own vocation at an incredibly early age. As she said in a 1960 newspaper interview, "I can remember, when I was a child, that all I ever wanted to do was to read and to write." She even wrote a short play at the age of eight. Later, in high school, she wrote "constantly."

Soon after graduating, her first poem was published, probably in a religious or educational periodical, and then she worked at writing in a very dedicated way for the rest of her life. In 1919, she married Loren Curry, a chemist, and they eventually had four children. But his work took them away from

Bushnell, to Bloomington, Peoria, Urbana, and eventually the Quad Cities, where he worked at the Rock Island Arsenal.

Curry's career gained momentum in the early 1930s, when she published poems in the *Chicago Tribune* and the *Washington D.C. Times-Herald* and in such periodicals as *The Instructor*, *The Children's Comrade*, *The Girl's Trend*, and *The Boy's Companion*. As those magazine titles suggest, some of her early poems are focused on childhood. One called "School Again!" captures the excitement of attending school for many small children:

Oh, I am so excited,
For September's come again;
I'm always glad, no matter how
Much fun the summer's been.
My books are new, my pencils, too;
My lunch is in my box.
It's such a lark to join my friends
And go to school in flocks.

Other childhood titles are "Learning How," "Roller Skating," "Up and Ready," and "The Bus Ride."

She wrote prose as well. Her first short story in a slick magazine was "Painting on Silk," about a troubled relationship from a female perspective, which appeared in *Home Journal* (May 1937). She wrote two one-act plays, *In for a Penny* (1936) and *What a Night!* (1942). The latter is described as "a mystery comedy." Her only novel, a murder mystery called *Come Sweet Death*, was published in London in 1937.

While many of her poems are not in dialect, all of her "ballads" about Bushnell are. A number of nineteenth-century American poets wrote in dialect—that is, in language characteristic of uneducated people. The most popular one was James Whitcomb Riley, whose poems of rural life, like "The Old Swimmin'-Hole" and "When the Frost is on the Punkin'," were often recited by schoolchildren of Curry's generation. He also focused intently on the world of childhood, as she later did.

Among her Bushnell dialect poems that were inspired by old-time cultural events and familiar places are "The Bushnell Fair" (an annual community festival, first held in 1879), "The Bushnell Horse Show" (an event that drew thousands of visitors, starting in 1908), "Ball's Skatin' Rink," and "Red Men's Hall." Perhaps the best one of that kind is "The Bushnell Opry House," which closes with a telling insight about small-town social life generations ago:

The Bushnell Opera House, built in 1883, became the focus of one of Curry's *Ballads of Bushnell.*

The Bushnell Horse Show drew huge crowds of spectators and horse buyers. Curry wrote a *Ballads of Bushnell* poem about that annual event.

The show don't make much difference,
If it be good or bad;
We laugh if it is funny, an'
We sniffle if it's sad.
The real fact is, we don't care
What it is all about.
Our fun is bein' all dressed up
An' seein' others out.

Some of her dialect poems reflect less prominent aspects of life in Bushnell that would otherwise be forgotten now. "Newsroom," for example, portrays the informal gatherings in "The back room o' Clark's drug store," and "Scottsburg Wood" depicts nut-gathering excursions in a forested area west of town. Perhaps the best of those poems, "Night Police," reflects two familiar figures from her childhood years:

One reason Bushnell felt so safe
When I was jest a tyke,
Jim Turner made the rounds at night
With his big bulldog, Mike....
No matter what the weather was,
Come rain, or sleet, or fog,
You'd allus see 'em walkin' round,
Jim Turner an' his dog.

Another interesting Bushnell dialect poem is "The Woman in Black," depicting the appearances of a local ghost, which created a huge sensation at the turn of the twentieth century. It was even written about in the Chicago newspapers. Perhaps it was a prankster dressed in black who had heard about a "woman in black" that had appeared in Colchester over the years and was out to frighten the Bushnell townspeople, but whatever the case, in Curry's childhood the ghost was a frightening and much-discussed phenomenon. "Draped in black an' actin' spooky," the "strange, m'sterious figger" that appeared so many times was even sought by groups of local men, but was never explained.

Curry died at Bettendorf in 1973. By the close of her writing career, which lasted until shortly before her death, she had published poems and stories in several dozen newspapers and magazines. Most of those works now seem dated and sentimentalized and have no readership. But her Bushnell dialect poems, which first appeared in the *McDonough Democrat* in the early 1940s and were soon printed together as *The Ballads of Bushnell*, continue to attract area readers. They are the chief literary legacy of the dedicated and sophisticated author whose community experience as a girl was inseparable from who she was and whose poetic memories of Bushnell have become an imperishable part of the county's past.

Martha K. Graham: Teacher and Writer

Another committed writer who also remembered the past was a gifted music teacher named Martha K. Graham, who not only produced poems throughout her life but several short memoirs as well. The best of her works are focused on small-town and rural life decades ago.

She was born in the village of Roseville, just north of the McDonough County border, in 1910. The town had many prosperous farming families with often imposing homes, but her father, Herbert King, was a blacksmith with a fifth-grade education. Martha always felt that she was destined to teach—perhaps because the family's small white house on the south edge of town was across the street from the local grade school and high school and her father's blacksmith shop was next to the library, where she spent many hours with books while waiting for him to finish his day's work.

Many years later, in a memoir called "Growing Up in Roseville, Illinois, in the Early 1900s," she recalled a secure, happy family life with literature and music: "My mother read stories and poems to us. Our parents played with us, [and] sang around the piano with us." Her mother played the piano for the Methodist church as well and always took young Martha to the choir practice.

Another crucial influence was her first-grade teacher, Julia Anderson, about whom she wrote, "I absorbed her intense interests in many things—art, poetry, music, reading, writing, nature, and teaching—all of which became important parts of my life. I loved her very much."

Roseville was not a culturally barren place like the stultifying Gopher Prairie in Sinclair Lewis's 1920 bestseller, *Main Street.* Graham especially recalled "good music teachers in the schools," who developed annual school musicals and well-attended recitals. Monmouth, not far away, had many programs too.

At age eighteen, Graham enrolled at Western Illinois State Teachers College in Macomb. In the two-year program there, she was influenced by English professors Irving Garwood and Mabel Corbin, who encouraged her to write; by biology professors Harry Waggoner and Roy Sallee, who led students on nature excursions around the lovely campus; and by music teachers Teresa Wild and Karl Crilly, who developed many student programs. Graham played the violin in a small college orchestra.

With a two-year diploma, she was hired to teach grades three and four in nearby Prairie City, a village of six hundred. Many years later, she wrote a superb memoir called "Living and Teaching in Prairie City, 1930–1935," which depicts a repressive social environment, especially regarding female teachers, who were prime targets for gossip and criticism. They had to conform to rigid rules of behavior, including mandatory church attendance and infrequent dating—outside of Prairie City only. When she started dating steadily another teacher, Burdette Graham, she was abruptly fired—essentially for falling in love. The two did marry, in August 1935, and he, of course, was allowed to remain on the faculty. Her memoir is an incisive exposé of narrow-minded small-town views about female teachers generations ago.

Graham went on to teach in country schools, some of which were far less repressive. One was Hatch School, near Avon, where she taught from 1935 to 1940. Another was Frog Pond School, just east of Macomb, where she remained for four years. As she later said in another memoir, "The Rural School Experience, 1936–1946," she loved it, despite the hard work: "I discovered that…I could do whatever I wanted, whenever I wanted to do it. That, perhaps, was the greatest joy of rural teaching. No one laid down arbitrary rules for me, no one rang bells to divide up the day, and no principal or other teacher came around, disapproving of what seemed to me legitimate noise and laughter." Her superb teaching there resulted in a 1945 article titled "They Learn and Have Fun at Frog Pond School" by nationally known writer John Strohm, which appeared in *The Prairie Farmer*. That was the most widely circulated report ever written about a country school in McDonough County.

And another kind of success was also coming. During Graham's Prairie City years, fate had placed her in the home of Mr. and Mrs. Arthur Decker, who took in "boarders." In 1937, their son James launched a publishing company devoted to poetry books. He eventually published over two hundred

Martha K. Graham and children at the Hatch School, where she taught after leaving Prairie City. Photograph taken in the later 1930s. *Courtesy of John Graham.*

titles, including two volumes by Edgar Lee Masters, *Illinois Poems* (1941) and *Along the Illinois* (1942).

Graham was already writing poetry, and with James Decker's encouragement she eventually produced two slim poetry paperbacks, *Prairie City Poems* and *Listen Forever*, which appeared in the early 1940s. The first was published under a pseudonym, Laurence Kinney, because she knew it was bound to cause a stir. Imitating Masters's *Spoon River Anthology*, she included several poetic monologues based on the lives of local people, as well as pieces like "Prairie City" and "East Cemetery." The speaker in the latter reflects the public's growing estrangement from pioneer culture:

Here they lie, the ones who lived and died
As pioneers—in this place set aside,
This quiet place, its lane grown up with grass,
Where Prairie City folks now seldom pass.

Another poem depicts the stress in earlier times on rural boys, especially poor ones, who had to balance the demands of schoolwork and farm work. It is a monologue titled "Thomas Andrews":

Those were the days a fellow fought to learn
To read and write, and figger, for to earn
Your board and bed by working in the field
Kept you out of class, with crops in yield,
And then you'd find yourself, a clumsy lout,
Put back with all the youngsters starting out.

One of the most effective monologues is "Matthew Harper" (later called "Fiddle-maker"), which depicts a man devoted to making and playing violins. As Graham revealed in a memoir written decades later, *Hes Phillips, Barber and Fiddle Maker*, her inspiration was a Prairie City businessman, a small-town virtuoso:

> *I was amazed to learn that he never had a formal music lesson in his life, yet he played a wooden flute, a trumpet, and a violin by ear and by note.... He especially liked stringed instruments, and in the back room of his barbershop he made violins in his spare time.... That was where he did his real work and lived his real life.*
>
> *As he handled his finished and unfinished violins, this quiet barber became a different person. The morose diffidence fell away, and I saw Hes Phillips as few people...must have ever known he could be. He simply loved everything about violins—the feel of them, the sound of them, playing them and making them.*

Her insightful memoir about the gifted but withdrawn man, whose barbershop later burned down, destroying most of his violin work, is a remarkable portrayal of an alienated and ultimately tragic figure, akin to the troubled small-town people in Sherwood Anderson's classic, *Winesburg, Ohio.*

In 1942, Graham produced a more substantial Decker Press volume called *Words for the Music.* A number of the poems, such as "Old Trysting Place," "Wild Geese," and "Oak Trees," dramatize the spiritual impact of the natural world on the attentive and sensitive speaker.

Later in the 1940s, Graham experienced the shocking end of the Decker Press. Faced with financial problems, Decker sold his publishing company, was later charged with embezzlement, and moved away. His sister Dorothy remained, working for a subsequent owner, Ervin Tax. In fact, the shy young woman fell in love with him, and in 1950, after it was clear that he had no real interest in her, she shot him in the head with a rifle and then killed herself. Some years later, for unrelated reasons, James Decker killed himself as well.

I was researching that sad episode when I got to know Martha Graham thirty years ago, and I asked her about the Deckers, the press, and the tragedy. She was helpful but would always avoid commenting on the psychological problems of those two tragic figures whom she had known so well. As she said, "Dorothy's violent death, along with that of the new owner, and later, James' similar death, I can scarcely think about."

In Macomb, she had continued her own drive for education, receiving from Western an MA degree in 1962 and a Certificate of Advanced Study in 1970. She taught school in Bushnell until 1976 and taught music to children in Macomb for over thirty years, becoming well known for her annual student recitals on themes like "Music is a Mirror," "Open Any Book," and "Once Upon a Time."

She continued to teach piano and organ lessons until 1993. She also continued to write poetry, some of it published by a company in Cedar Rapids, Iowa. But by late in her life, her most important literary works were memoirs. Our acquaintance developed when I published several in *Tales from Two Rivers* collections, including "Hes Phillips, Barber and Fiddle Maker," and I printed in a newsletter her superb piece on "Living and Teaching in Prairie City, 1930–1935," which includes a character sketch of James Decker.

When Martha Graham died in 2002, at age ninety-one, McDonough County lost a great crusader for books and music in the lives of children and a talented reflector of rural and small-town life generations ago. Her inner growth and her splendid career are testaments to the impact of dedicated teachers.

Don O'Harra: Last of the Old-Time Country Printers

With the passing of Don O'Harra on March 15, 2009, at the age of ninety-three, an era in our county's history, and perhaps in our state's, has come to a close: the era of "the old-time country printer." He had become, in fact, the historian, the eulogist, and the living symbol of that tradition, which stretched back to pioneer days. What was absolutely central to it was not the fascination with writing or the yearning to inform, but the love of small-town life, the desire to appreciate it, foster it, and maintain it against all odds.

Don developed that love partly because he was so deeply connected to pre-modern Macomb, the old tight-knit, semi-isolated community where everyone knew everyone else, and belonging was a way of life.

His father was Ira O'Harra, who was raised in the village of Bentley (in Hancock County) during the 1870s and 1880s and who became a Macomb lawyer in 1897. Soon respected by his peers and popular with the public, he was mayor of Macomb in 1913 and 1914. That was just before Don was born. He grew up in the big house his father built on North Randolph Street, later the Inselhaus bed-and-breakfast, where town leaders were frequent visitors and community issues were part of everyday conversation.

After graduating from the University of Illinois, Don moved to New York City, where he learned typesetting and worked for McGraw-Hill Publishing Company. The Depression was still on, and he was glad to have a job. A few years later, World War II started, and he joined up. After four years in the service, he returned to McGraw-Hill, where he met and married New Yorker Hilda Howe, herself a trained printer.

The main street in Bardolph during the 1940s, when Don O'Harra edited the local newspaper.

At about that time, Don told his father, "I'd like to edit a small-town weekly," and Ira soon mentioned that veteran small-town newspaperman Harry Maxwell was thinking of selling the *Bardolph News.* So Don and Hilda bought it and headed for Illinois. That was in 1946, when downtown Bardolph consisted of "the grocery, the post office, an empty building, the pool room, the printshop, the telephone office, and Holcomb's Garage on the corner," as Don later put it. And within that village culture, he soon realized, "*The Bardolph News* really belonged." Indeed, Harry Maxwell's older brother had established the *News* in 1896, and Harry had worked there during childhood, then taught school, and then owned the newspaper himself for three decades. Known as "a brilliant writer and editor," he became a mentor for Don and a link to the country printer tradition.

A quarter century ago, not long after I started the *McDonough County Historical Society Newsletter*, I asked Don to write about his postwar years at the *Bardolph News*, and he produced a fascinating memoir. As he recalled, "The machinery was old letterpress printing equipment. Foundry type, mostly of lead, was heavy.... And the newspaper press, an old Potter, had been brought from LaHarpe to Bardolph by oxen."

For all their big-city expertise, Don and Hilda were newspaper neophytes, and they knew it. "While my wife and I knew about design, paper, print quality, and the graphic arts," he said, "we had much to learn from an old editor, who knew the county like a book." Deeply rooted, Harry Maxwell knew a thousand stories about local folks, including some he could never print.

Anxious to succeed, Don discovered that "the best reporters which a small newspaper has are its readers," and fortunately, the old "party phone line" at the newspaper office made that easy. As he later said, "One could just lift the receiver and get all kinds of news. No one objected to my breaking in to a conversation to confirm a fact."

Don soon learned that the old-style village newspaper was a great promoter of community life as well as an outlet for writing talent if you liked to appreciate people. And he did. As he once put it, "Only in *The Bardolph News* was there a column called 'Harvest of the Grim Reaper.' I realized that an obituary article was an opportunity for me to write a profile that couldn't be bettered in the *New Yorker* magazine. And I found out that it would sell newspapers."

After four tough years in a village that continued to decline, the O'Harras moved the heavy Intertype machine (akin to Linotype) and press to a somewhat bigger town and started the *Colchester Chronicle*. There, too, the local news consisted mostly of "births, deaths, accidents, and gatherings," as Don later said, but he printed occasional articles with a historical focus, too, and promoted the 1956 Colchester Centennial celebration. Also, he printed June Moon's popular paperback history of the town.

A decade later, the O'Harras discontinued that small-circulation paper and simply did job printing, but several years after Hilda died, Don started the *Chronicle* once again, in 1975. He was then sixty years old.

Soon after that, I got to know him. We had in common a fascination with small-town folks, a love of local history, a sense that community in America was fading, and an urge to chronicle people and things that were forever passing away. As Don talked of his work at the *Chronicle*, I realized that there wasn't much money in it, that he had revived the weekly paper simply because he loved small-town life, wanted to maintain a sense of community in Colchester, and by then, realized that he was the last of a dying breed, an old country editor who had links back to Linotype machines and beyond, back to "the 100 drawers of metal typeface," the "printer's type sticks," the composing table, and the sheet-fed press that he had acquired with the *Bardolph News* office. He felt connected to a tradition.

Don O'Harra standing in front of the *Colchester Chronicle* office in the 1950s.

In his later years, Don occasionally spoke and wrote about the long newspaper history of McDonough County, and he readily shared his insider's view of the small-town weekly, a "once-cherished local phenomenon," as he said, that he knew was disappearing here and elsewhere across America. He wrote a three-part series, "Weekly Newspapers of McDonough County," for the *Historical Society Newsletter* in 1998, and as recently as 2008 he wrote another newsletter article on "Printing as It Was Done in Our County," which explained the exacting process of setting type by hand and printing on a flatbed press.

Don's career and his commitment as the last of the old-time country printers in this area, a man who gave up a good job in America's publishing capital to edit two of our last village newspapers, is a great small-town story. And it has a certain statewide significance too. In a reference book on Illinois newspapers, I looked up the *Colchester Chronicle* during the early 1980s, and the statistics there confirmed what I had long suspected: With only about four hundred subscribers, the *Chronicle* was the smallest-circulation newspaper in the state of Illinois.

I was working at the Western Illinois University Archives then, trying hard, in a desperate race against destruction, to collect and preserve all the historical documents and photographs I could get my hands on in the sixteen-county western Illinois region, and nobody in all those counties was more helpful than Don O'Harra. He even started seeking from his readers old Colchester-area photographs for printing in the *Chronicle*, and whenever he got one, he would call me and lend it so I could copy it for the archives. The Colchester Collection at the WIU Library is immensely indebted to him. He was also busy then helping to found the Colchester Public Library, and he later (in 1993) co-founded the Colchester Area Historical Society and was the organization's longtime secretary.

Don also told me stories about the old days in McDonough County, back when he was a kid, and he even passed along a few tales that he had heard from the old-timers in Colchester about a certain bootlegger named Kelly Wagle. In fact, Don lived next door to the bootlegger's elderly widow, Blanche. He cautioned me to stay away from her, to dig out that small-town crime story (which became *The Bootlegger*) on the sly, and not tip Blanche off that I was working on it—and to assure all of my local informants that I'd never reveal who told me anything. So he could be a good mentor, too, as well as a precious link with the local past. He knew his townspeople, knew their values, knew what really mattered to them.

And speaking of links with the past, Don eventually married one. Many years after Hilda had died, he married Laura Sweany, a Macomb native who had been living for many years in Michigan. She was a widow then and, like Don, was in her later sixties. Don and Laura had been childhood playmates and teenage friends, so they had a lot of common memories of get-togethers and old-timers, holidays and schooldays, and they had a similar sense of deep belonging.

They married in 1984, and of course, Laura was soon helping with the *Colchester Chronicle*. When they finally sold it to Stacey Nicholas and Joe Coelho in 1994, Don and Laura continued to work there just to help out. But the *Chronicle* too eventually folded. Then the O'Harras moved to Macomb, where they were a familiar sight at local historical society meetings. Their late-in-life marriage lasted for a quarter of a century.

Over the generations, McDonough County has been fortunate to have a long series of talented and dedicated small-town newspaper editors, including such notable figures as B.R. Hampton, W.H. Hainline, Van Hampton, and Harry Maxwell. And no one cared more about that tradition than Don O'Harra, the last of the old-time country printers, who spoke for them all.

Part II
Places in the Heart

Dealing with Death: The Old Macomb Cemetery

Of the many historic places in McDonough County, perhaps the most underappreciated is the Old Macomb Cemetery, west of town, on Wigwam Hollow Road. It is also one of the most fascinating.

When the first burials occurred there, Andrew Jackson was president, Abraham Lincoln was at New Salem, and Chief Black Hawk was still refusing to leave his native land to the whites, who kept coming and coming and coming. This was the edge of the frontier, the Far West.

According to S.J. Clarke's *History of McDonough County*, during 1830 Peter Hale built a log cabin on the quarter section of land where the graveyard was soon established. A private burial ground was started on the crest of the hill later that year, after a little girl in the Hale family (apparently their only child) fell into a fire and was burned to death. No headstone remains to mark her grave site or record her name, but she was the first of more than three hundred people buried at that location.

There are, however, some 190 remaining grave markers, many of them old, which provide a kind of historic background to the surrounding residential area, which slopes northward to the Lamoine River. They provoke the infrequent cemetery visitor to reflect on the past—and confront the reality of death.

Altogether, twenty-eight people who were born prior to 1800 are buried at the Old Macomb Cemetery. Because most of them died before the county had a newspaper, they will always be obscure figures—their lives mysteriously entangled with the westward movement that brought settlers to the Prairie State.

The slate headstone of Cyrus A. Walker (namesake of the famous lawyer) in the Old Macomb Cemetery is one of many with poetic inscriptions.

One of those older pioneers, about whom we know very little, is Robert Garrett, who was born in 1770 and died at age eighty-five. According to Macomb historian Alex Holmes, in 1835 Garrett bought the graveyard land (two acres) from pioneer merchant William Bailey and Dr. Charles Hays, who had bought it from Hale, and he sold it one year later to the county for use as a public burial ground. Conscious of his own approaching death, he may have been responsible for the formal establishment of the cemetery.

Garrett's modest gravestone has a version of the most common early American poetic epitaph:

Behold, you strangers passing by,
As you are now so once was I.
As I am now so you shall be;
Prepare for death and follow me.

That striking epitaph belongs to a New England religious tradition that preceded the Revolutionary War, and it was often accompanied by a carved death's-head. The lines are effective because the voice of the dead person speaks directly to the onlooker, reversing their roles and, ironically, living through the epitaph while reminding the graveyard visitor of his own mortality. It is precisely such mingling of individual lives with mankind's universal predicament that gives cemeteries, especially old ones, their unique impact. The reflective visitor develops an increased sense of his own temporality. He, too, is headed for the graveyard.

In contrast, the poetic inscription on James Moore's headstone sweeps the reader into another realm, poised between time and eternity, life and afterlife, as the dead speaker affirms the Christian promise:

God my redeemer lives
And ever from the skies
Looks down and watches all my dust
Till he shall bid it rise.

That comment from the grave suggests the profound cultural meaning of "cemetery." It is not just a burying ground for bodies but a place where lives are recalled with stones and epitaphs—and where the metaphysical assumptions held by some people have a surface reality that you can experience.

Moore's 1841 slate headstone is signed at the bottom with the initials "J.L." It is, then, a marker produced by pioneer stone carver John Long, whose work makes the Old Macomb Cemetery one of the most unique burying grounds in western Illinois. When I brought his grave markers to public attention in 1983, very little was known about him, but since then, an outline of his life has begun to emerge.

Born in Glasgow, Scotland, on March 14, 1812, Long immigrated to America with his parents, who settled in Maryland. Exactly when he came to McDonough County is unknown, but he married a pioneer's daughter, Corinthy Twitchell, in 1834, and they settled on ten acres just a mile north of Macomb, along Crooked Creek, near the old Burlington Road. Aside from cutting and carving local gravestones, he worked for a year on the Mormon Temple at Nauvoo during the early 1840s. Most notable among his projects was a drawing, a plan he developed, for the massive baptismal font, which rested on twelve stone oxen, and he also helped to produce that sculpture. But Long apparently became disenchanted with his employer—and perhaps spiritual leader—Joseph Smith, for he later served as a captain in the McDonough County militia during the Mormon War. Soon afterward, he served for a year in the Mexican War, fighting at the Battle of Monterrey. Mustered out in May 1847, he returned to McDonough County, where he died that September from unknown causes at age thirty-five. Presumably, he was buried in the Old Macomb Cemetery, but ironically, there is no headstone or definite record. His widow and children soon moved to Utah with relatives, and there she remarried. Ironically, too, they became, or remained, Mormons.

In the old cemetery, Long's name or initials appear on half a dozen headstones, but he clearly made some that were never signed, for his lettering reflects an old style that is rare in the Midwest and is easy to recognize, and his markers often have borders and inscriptions. Also, the Long headstones have a variation of the curved top, or "headboard," shape common to the early East Coast, where he surely learned his trade.

Long's briefest sermon in stone appears on the marker for George W. Mead, who "departed this life" in 1839: "Youth behold the grave/ and living, learn to die." That grim headstone is signed "J.L." But not far away is the 1844 marker for Mead's mother, Lydia, which is unsigned but has every characteristic of Long's work, including a brief, pointed epitaph: "She has gone to heaven/ to enjoy that peace/ which fate denied her here." Most of the Old Macomb Cemetery epitaphs are surely not original, but this one may be, for it reflects the dead woman's spiritual struggle, as well as the family's confidence in her salvation. Her headstone reminds us of the personal dramas that are hidden beneath the sod in every graveyard.

Although there will always be mysteries about the life of John Long and uncertainty about how many grave markers he did produce, he was an uncommonly talented craftsman in stone, much appreciated by the local pioneers who employed him to create memorial markers—and help them deal with death. His hand-carved headstones are the oldest historical artifacts in McDonough County that can be connected with the person who produced them, and they lend a quaint character to the long unused pioneer burial ground. They also prompt us to reflect on our own mortality and our generation's place in the flow of time.

Pennington Point: The Old Days in a Rural Hamlet

Pennington Point is now a ghost town—or perhaps a ghost hamlet, since it never was much of a town. For decades, however, it was a community center for rural folks in southeastern McDonough County. On the frontier, it was located near a stretch of timber that came to a point on the gently rolling prairie of New Salem Township. Now the few community buildings are gone, and the place is marked only by a very well-kept, historic cemetery, noted for its graves of nineteenth-century soldiers.

The first settler in that area was William Pennington, a native of Virginia who arrived on January 1, 1828. He left after a year or so, later building a homestead in Emmet Township, but in 1830 a relative came to occupy that New Salem Township land—and stayed for many years. He was Stewart Pennington, for whom the frontier settlement was named in 1834. Stewart was the son of Richard and Hannah (Boone) Pennington and the nephew of America's most famous frontiersman, Daniel Boone. He died in 1859 and is buried in the old cemetery.

The second settler, Salem Woods, was a native of New York. In 1828, he walked all the way from Pennsylvania to locate and examine his already-purchased land, and then he settled there permanently in 1831. In an interview shortly before his death in 1879, he recalled his arduous trip to McDonough County, which brought him to the county's first community, Carter's Settlement—located along the trail leading up from Rushville—on his way to the remote, pathless wilds of New Salem Township.

Another early settler was Wesley Harlan, who came during the later 1830s. In 1926, his tenth child, Chloe Hall, reconstructed from memory

A contemporary photograph of the well-kept Pennington Point Cemetery, which has a historical marker near the entrance.

and family tradition her father's early work as a miller and carpenter, which clearly helped to make the Pennington Point area well known among nearby pioneers:

> *Father* [eventually] *built the grist mill and the carpenter shop. The mill was all of his own making, save the great grinding stones.... Men came from miles away, all over the prairie, bringing wheat and corn and buckwheat to be ground there. Father would bring out four big horses and hitch them to the beam that turned the big wheel and set the stones to grinding out the grist. For hours and hours my brother and I would sit on the beam, riding round and round....*
>
> *In winter Father worked in his shop, making cupboards, bedsteads, chairs, and all kinds of household furniture.... I wish I might have shown* [you] *the spinning wheel, winding blades, hackle, and loom which he made for my mother, and which enabled her to manufacture not only clothing for the family but also carpets, blankets, and household linen—in fact, all the fabrics we used. He also made sleds, wagons, and many other farm implements.*

Her memory of riding on the beam reveals how deeply rooted she was in the unmechanized world that had, by 1926, long since passed away.

One of Chloe's brothers, George Harlan, kept a diary during the 1850s, and the young bachelor noted that community life in those days centered on the one-room school, where spelling matches, debates, and speeches were important cultural and social events. Quilting bees and corn huskings were also popular. And, of course, the whole neighborhood attended marriages and funerals together.

The most interesting figure in early Pennington Point was perhaps Stephen Yocum, who came from Kentucky. A militia captain in early southern Illinois, he was later a soldier in the Black Hawk War, commissioned as a major by Governor Reynolds, and during that conflict he became acquainted with fellow Kentuckian Abraham Lincoln. In the 1830s, Yocum had enough money to acquire five hundred acres of land, on which he built a log cabin, and in 1850 he constructed a two-story frame house, which had five bedrooms and featured four fireplaces. It was the largest home in Pennington Point.

Yocum was noted for his integrity, humanity, and generosity. In 1862, one of the first black families to live in McDonough County came to Yocum's farm seeking a place to settle. Milford and Dicey Daniels, as slaves in Kentucky, had once known the Yocum family. It is not clear whether they escaped from the South with their several children or had been able to buy their freedom, but they came seeking help—at a time when blacks were unwelcome in McDonough County. Major Yocum gave them four acres of ground, provided a cabin, and helped them to become established at Pennington Point, where Daniels worked as a farm laborer. That family later moved to Macomb.

A likeable, good-natured person, Yocum was also noted for his sense of humor. A religious skeptic, he once quipped, to mark the difference between his churchgoing wife and himself, "She is the praying kind, and I am the paying kind." A tall, handsome obelisk now marks the major's grave in the local cemetery.

Yocum and his wife, Mary, had nine daughters and only two sons. One of those boys died as a child, and the other, George, was killed in the Civil War at the Battle of Stone's River, on December 31, 1862. He was the color sergeant (flag bearer) of the Eighty-fourth Infantry Regiment and, hence, was targeted by the Rebel sharpshooters. Few McDonough County deaths in the war were more heroically reported. His body was never recovered, but the bereaved family placed a marker for him in the cemetery.

There are twenty-six other Union soldiers buried at Pennington Point—and, oddly enough, one Confederate soldier. Among the other noted graves is that of Mickey Hammond, who fought in the War of 1812 as a young man in Tennessee. He was perhaps the last McDonough County veteran of that conflict to pass away, dying in 1880. He had been venerated as an old hero, so his funeral was widely attended.

Post–Civil War Pennington Point had a church, a country school, a general store, a post office, a blacksmith shop, and a doctor's office, as well as half a dozen homes. After Stephen Yocum died in 1874, the most well-known local figure was Simon Raby, who operated the blacksmith shop and the store and was also the postmaster for many years.

Several developments ultimately doomed the rural community. For one thing, a railroad never came through there. The CB&Q and TP&W both crossed the county farther north. The post office was finally closed in 1902, and the general store vanished soon afterward.

The most important institution in the hamlet's history was the Methodist church, which sustained the identity of Pennington Point. It had been organized in 1835, and the first church building had been located a mile south of the cemetery, but a second, white-frame structure, built in 1877, was moved to a site by the cemetery in 1896. Religious revivals were often held there, and it served as a community center. In fact, the church held an annual fish fry, starting in 1927, which drew people from a wide area.

But the church was destroyed by fire in 1943. It was replaced by another church, moved to that site in 1947, but the congregation dwindled, and the last services were held there in 1968. The building was torn down four years later, and now only a monument to the church, including the old bell, remains at the site.

Pennington Point is no longer a rural community, just a lovely spot in the countryside where people once created frontier farms, established a few commercial enterprises, labored and learned, struggled and suffered, raised their families, and passed away. But there is a precious unity about the place, for most of the former local residents, once so deeply interconnected, remain together in the old burying ground.

Hills Grove and Rattlesnake Den Hollow

Another notable hamlet in nineteenth-century McDonough County was Hills Grove, located in Tennessee Township near the Hancock County border. Started in the early 1830s, it soon became noted for three things: a pioneer who was a moral role model, a log cabin "seminary" (or school of higher learning), and a long, rocky, dangerous ravine called Rattlesnake Den Hollow.

The earliest settler was an affable, kindly, socially committed frontiersman named Roswell Tyrrell, who hailed from Connecticut, by way of Ohio. While just a teenager, he had served in the War of 1812, and not long afterward, in 1819, he had traveled to the new state of Illinois. He was perhaps the earliest resident of Illinois to eventually settle within the county's borders. First located in southern Illinois, he moved in 1823 to Fulton County, and then in 1830 to McDonough, where he built a log cabin at what would become Hills Grove. The "winter of the deep snow" kept him from bringing his family there until the spring of 1831.

Like Stephen Yocum in Pennington Point, Tyrrell was not a churchgoer, but his sensitive commitment to others made him a legendary figure. His lengthy biographical sketch in the 1885 *History of McDonough County* portrays him as a kind of secular saint:

> *Mr. Tyrrell was never a member of a church, though in life he was a strictly moral man. The second great commandment, to "love thy neighbor as thyself," he carried out to the letter….*

> *During the dark days of the war, he was intensely loyal…and many acts of kindness did he perform for the dear ones left behind. No wife, sister, or mother of a soldier would be allowed to suffer if it was in his power to minister relief….*
>
> *He had a heart overflowing with love of humanity, and to the poor he was ever kind and considerate. The cabin which he erected in 1830, it is said, was the first home of every family in the Hills Grove settlement, and not a cent of rent was he ever known to receive for its use. If the family was poor, or in need of any of the necessaries of life, Uncle Roswell was ever ready to supply their wants. A sack of flour or meal, or a ham of meat, or whatever might be the object of their need, was dropped quietly at their door.*

Tyrrell was also legendary for his honesty and integrity—so much so that a common remark about some person's ethical behavior in western McDonough County was that "Uncle Roswell Tyrrell couldn't do better than that."

Tyrrell was neither wealthy nor influential, but his biographical sketch was probably the only one that ever got into that massive county history by popular demand, for the author asserted that everywhere he went in western McDonough County, "nearly every person we met inquired of us if we did not intend to give a sketch of the life of Uncle Roswell Tyrrell," and he concluded that "his memory is held in grateful remembrance by hundreds of the old citizens of the county." A shared awareness of the venerated pioneer had become an important cultural bond.

Tyrrell's death in 1872, when he was almost seventy-three years old, was widely lamented. He had obviously played an important, if informal, role in promoting community life at the hamlet of Hills Grove, which had at the time of his death a blacksmith shop and a general store, as well as a post office and a doctor. By then, a dozen homes were in or near the tiny town.

The most noted institution in early Hills Grove was not a church (although the Methodists organized early), but a school, and the founder of it matched Roswell Tyrrell in local importance by giving the hamlet a certain focus and distinction. Moreover, he too was a man of enormous social commitment.

Isaac Holton was born on March 13, 1790, in Westminster, Vermont, and he was surely the most well-educated man in early McDonough County. During his teens he attended the academy (the equivalent of a high school) at Deerfield, Massachusetts, and then attended the University of Vermont,

A nineteenth-century painting of Isaac Holton, who built the Hills Grove Seminary in 1837.

graduating in 1814. After a brief career as a lawyer, he started teaching, and soon served as the principal (or main teacher) at academies in several Maine and Vermont towns. Although he left no statement of his motive for coming to McDonough County, he was clearly a social idealist, committed to enhancing life in the Far West through education. His daughter, Julia Ferris, writing of him in 1925, referred to his "interest in the children and young people" and "his plan for the betterment of conditions" in early Hills Grove. Fortunately, she also depicted the family's trip west and their crude log cabin home:

> *In September, 1835, he* [Isaac] *left Vermont, with his family* [wife Phoebe and four children], *accompanied also by his brother, William, whose children, John and Isabel, came with him.... With a one-horse wagon driven by the nephew and a two-horse wagon which contained supplies for the trip and the new home, they undertook the long and perilous journey, lasting fourteen weeks, reaching their future home on December 15, 1835. They found on the land an unoccupied log cabin, of which they took possession. It was perhaps eighteen feet square, one room, with a clapboard roof, a puncheon floor,* [and] *no windows, light coming in only by the door when open. A little light came through the poorly chinked logs, and Mother said she could see the stars through holes in the roof.*

She also described her father's "Hills Grove Seminary." It was a log cabin schoolhouse, which Holton built with the help of neighbors "as soon after he came to Illinois as he could interest people in the [better education] movement" that was his mission. It was completed by 1837. In fact, Julia Ferris provides the most detailed description of a log cabin school that survives from McDonough County:

> *The seminary, as we called the school building, was a one-story structure with a loft above, 20 x 24 feet on the ground.... The floor was of split logs hewn flat with ax and adze, of the type called puncheon.... The seats were of logs split, with auger holes bored in the rounded side for wooden legs.... There was a desk on a raised platform, where Father sat as a teacher, keeping rather strict discipline, as I well remember. This desk was used as a pulpit on Sundays....*
>
> *My father taught the common branches* [i.e., primary subjects] *to the children of the neighborhood, but he also had a class of young men whom he was instructing in languages, in mathematics, and other subjects, preparing them for college....*
>
> *The seminary was also used on Sunday for church and Sunday school, as well as for all other community gatherings. The room was lighted by candles in those early days.*

Of course, Holton and other settlers from the East Coast were often viewed with suspicion in a county dominated by Kentucky-Tennessee pioneers, and perhaps for that reason, rumors later circulated that escaping slaves were hidden in the school's loft. That is doubtful, although Holton, Tyrrell, Charles Gilchrist (from New Hampshire), and other Hills Grove "Yankees" were opposed to slavery. In any case, it is clear that Holton's school also served as a community center, which was part of his social plan.

A revered teacher and local leader who created the town plat in 1844, Holton remained at Hills Grove for a dozen years, and then he moved to Carthage, at the invitation of school officials there, but illness soon ended his career. He and Phoebe then returned to the beloved hamlet, the chosen place, where his school had been located and his vision of community had been fostered. He died in 1850, and she passed away much later, in 1887. His "seminary," the earliest post-primary school in McDonough County, became a district school during the 1850s, but it "was crowded to its utmost capacity," according to a teacher of that era, so Holton's effort to place education at the center of community life apparently had a lasting impact at Hills Grove.

By the time Isaac Holton died, the hamlet was also noted for a wild area named Rattlesnake Den Hollow, which began near the Hills Grove schoolhouse and cemetery and descended for most of two miles to the southwest before connecting with Crooked Creek just across the Hancock County border. Among the rock formations there is Balanced Rock, sitting high on a bluff. Perhaps the rugged nature of that terrain—the most remote area in McDonough County—accounts for the various wild animal stories that survive from Hills Grove's pioneer days. In the early twentieth century, for example, Thomas Webb recalled his parents' encounter with a lynx in the woods, well before the Civil War. Later, hunters apparently killed a lynx and two panthers as well. Also, William S. Owen told how his grandparents, who first came in 1832, pursued and killed a black bear on the land where they settled. That is the only record of a bear in McDonough County.

But the most notorious wild creatures there were rattlesnakes. As Owen also pointed out, "Rattlesnakes…were plentiful and did much harm, biting people and killing stock, Abram Fulkerson [his great uncle] being one who was bitten by a rattler which later caused his death." According to an early naturalist and student of the county's Indian prehistory, Charles Harris, who wrote about the area in 1921, the Hills Grove settlers initiated "a war of extermination" after Abram Fulkerson's death:

> *It was found that a rocky ravine* [Rattlesnake Den Hollow]…*was their winter home, crevasses in the rock ledges furnishing them shelter. For two seasons guards watched the entrances to the dens during the spring, when the warming sun was drawing the snakes out,* [to kill them]…*but on a third spring a live trap was invented, which only had to be visited every few days to remove and destroy its catch.*
>
> *As many as nine hundred snakes were destroyed in a single season, but this included many of the harmless varieties, black snakes especially…. So thoroughly was the work done that snakes are rare in the ravine today, and I think no rattlers have been seen there for many years.*

More complete information about the struggle with snakes at the big ravine is probably beyond recovery, but that pioneer effort gave Rattlesnake Den Hollow its name—and supplied the hamlet of Hills Grove with a host of snake stories that lasted for generations.

Now the only structure identified with Hills Grove is the Methodist church, but it wasn't built until 1891, after the community was already in decline, so it does not reflect the hamlet's early heritage. More historic is the isolated but well-kept cemetery, on the very edge of Rattlesnake Den Hollow, where many of the local pioneers are buried. Among them are the two "Yankees," Roswell Tyrrell and Isaac Holton, who were models of social commitment and deserve to be remembered despite the fading of their little town.

The Legendary Place Called Gin Ridge

Of all the place names associated with McDonough County, past or present, Gin Ridge is the only one that has meaning that is not strictly geographical. Although identified on some county maps as a location in Bethel Township, it has for generations also designated a point of view—rural, unsophisticated, and independent. And decades ago it was also synonymous with lower-class character and values, especially drunken behavior and brawling, so that to call someone a "Gin Ridger" was an insult.

The history of Gin Ridge has gone largely unrecorded, but there is enough information about the area to reveal the kind of culture that developed there—and to suggest why it came to have that special, legendary significance.

Bethel Township, half timber and half prairie, in south central McDonough County, was settled primarily by frontier families who had come from Kentucky and Tennessee. No doubt the various ridges in the southern part of that township—and northern Schuyler County—reminded those pioneers of the landscape they had left behind. Among the early Gin Ridge families were the Frakes, McCoys, Miners, Sapps, Shoopmans, Stonekings, Tolands, Wheelers, and Willeys. The Stonekings later owned virtually all of the ridge, and Andrew and Rachel Stoneking operated the sole commercial enterprise, the Gin Ridge Store, from the late nineteenth century to the Depression.

However, most of the early settlers were poor folks accustomed to living in log cabins, cultivating small fields of wheat and corn, raising a few hogs

The Gin Ridge Store operated from the early twentieth century until the 1930s.

and chickens, and hunting to supplement their diet. James Sapp recalled that his father, Brommel Sapp, "came to the Ridge with a family of ten children…and with all his earthly possessions stored in a one-horse wagon, pulled by a blind mare."

Historical records about those settlers are hard to come by, but toward the end of the century, M.A. Wheeler recalled that "early days on the Ridge were noted for log-cabin raising, buckskin…to make clothing of, plows with wooden moleboards, deer, wolves, and other wild game…and above all else, the best of good feeling between neighbors." As that suggests, the Gin Ridge area exhibited the typical characteristics of southern upland frontier culture.

More important, it retained that identity long after other rural areas of McDonough and Schuyler Counties had developed large, prosperous farms and had organized schools and churches for the improvement of local society. An early article on the Gin Ridge area of northern Schuyler County, published in 1859, refers to the lack of good schools and churches: "Their school facilities are bad; some send over to McDonough, and others over to a schoolhouse on Fizzle Ridge, two or three miles distant. Those inclined to go to church attend at Doddsville, Brooklyn, or some of the other towns around."

Residents of Gin Ridge also developed a reputation for drinking and fighting—especially in the eyes of their more community-oriented, churchgoing neighbors to the north, at Macomb. That reputation was no doubt unfairly popularized by the name "Gin Ridge," which nearby temperance advocates must have associated with the evils of liquor. Yet there was some real truth to it, as historical records suggest.

In July 1879, for example, the following item was written by the Gin Ridge correspondent of the *Macomb Journal*: "Charley and Dump Jewel went to Augusta, to spend the 4th. While on the road home, both being under the influence of whisky, Dump got out of the wagon, and Charles went to help him into the wagon, and then Dump stabbed him in the abdomen, and Charles died in five minutes."

The writer of that piece did not mention that, in fact, there were five Gin Ridgers involved in that fracas, "all more or less intoxicated," according to another article. One of the others was also severely wounded. Enoch "Dump" Jewel confessed to the killing and was sentenced to prison.

It is not surprising that an 1896 *Macomb Journal* article, perhaps by W.H. Hainline, characterized the issue of stature among the men of Gin Ridge along those same lines: "In years gone by, it was not a question with the men who lived there as to who had the most to eat or wear, or who owned the most land, but who had come nearest to killing a man without actually doing it, who was the best fighter, the best wrestler—or who could drink the most 'red licker.'" The writer of that piece even reported that "it was generally conceded that the Stonekings were the 'best,' but the Willeys made them a close second."

As the years passed, the limits of Gin Ridge began to expand. By the late 1850s, the name had become synonymous with all of Bethel Township, so that one writer of that era could remark, "Middletown…is sometimes jocosely called 'the Capital of Gin Ridge.'" Middletown was the early name of Fandon, founded in 1837 in the northwest corner of the township. The village originated as a stage stop midway between Beardstown and Burlington, and according to an 1853 description in the *McDonough Independent*, it contained at that time "180 inhabitants—three dry goods stores, three taverns, several blacksmith shops, and a splendid steam saw mill." In spite of being miles away to the north, Middletown had cultural connections with the Ridge, for it was a southern upland, whisky-drinking kind of a community.

By the post–Civil War years, Gin Ridge had come to represent, in the public mind, a rural community (or entire township) of poor, self-reliant people—a sort of permanent frontier that remained rough, rowdy, and uncultured while the rest of McDonough County strove to improve. It had become a kind of anti-Macomb in the minds of many. The county seat was orderly, progressive, cultured, and increasingly Republican. Gin Ridge was the opposite: disorderly, backward, rustic, and—worst of all—staunchly Democratic.

That difference was exploited by a satirist who became Macomb's first locally popular writer. He used the pseudonym "Pawl Pry," which was based on the title character in a play called *Paul Pry* (1825) by British dramatist John Poole. Due to the popularity of that comic farce, the name "Paul Pry" was used to denote any inquisitive, meddlesome individual. The Macomb author deliberately misspelled the name, for his letters to the *Journal* were written in an artificial colloquial dialect, characterized by poor spelling, which denoted his mouthpiece character's lack of education.

Those Pawl Pry columns were modeled on the nationally famous Petroleum V. Nasby articles. Nasby was the pseudonym, or fictional creation, of David Ross Locke, editor of the *Toledo Blade*. In the person of Petroleum V. Nasby, Locke created the satiric archetype of everything bad about post–Civil War America, and his dialect satires appeared in many newspapers from the 1860s to the 1880s, including the *Macomb Journal*. When I first wrote about Pawl Pry a quarter century ago, I did not know the author's real identity, but I later discovered that he was B.R. Hampton, who edited Macomb newspapers from 1855 until his death in 1886 and was co-editor of the *Journal* during the 1870s.

The Pawl Pry columns began appearing in 1871. The early ones were devoted to political satire, aimed at the Democrats, but in the fall of 1873, Hampton moved his satirical commentator back to Gin Ridge, and the focus of his satire began to shift. Pry became a spokesman for the Gin Ridgers—not to ridicule them, but to criticize economic and political forces that oppressed the working man, "the laboring people uv Gin Ridge," during the depression years that marked the 1870s. For example, in the following passage from an 1878 article, Pawl Pry complains of inequities:

> *I am still here a-doin the best I kin to make a livin, tho I find it rite hard work to maik things cum out even.... I never cood see enny jest reson why wun class uv men shood rule in lucksury and hev every thing they want while others ken get skeercely enuff tu keep sole and boddy together. Wun*

> *man has millions uv gold, whilst thousands hevent got a nickel.... There is sumpthing radikly rong in the way things is arranged, and if there isent sum change maid, and the welth of the nashen more equably distribooted, the people hev not yet seen the bottom uv the hard times.*

The Pawl Pry columns continued to appear in the *Macomb Journal* until the early 1880s, proclaiming the importance of the Gin Ridge perspective—that is, the viewpoint of the poor, unsophisticated, laboring man. During that time, Pry emerged as a figure who was not very wise in the ways of the world, and certainly not educated, but who was nevertheless earnest, hardworking, and sensitive to the needs of poor rural people like himself. And Gin Ridge, of course, became recognized wherever the *Journal* circulated.

It is not surprising to find that, in 1890, Macomb lawyer and traveling newspaper correspondent W.W. Vose referred to Gin Ridge as a "mythical country" with a wide reputation. Indeed, it was—and not only because the actual ridge was notoriously difficult to locate, being always "just a little farther on." For by that time, Gin Ridge was widely known, not as a real place in the McDonough County countryside but as a symbolic location—a cultural backwater somewhere south of prosperity, where the American Dream had never arrived.

The Old Fairground and the Times that Were

McDonough County has not held fairs for many years, but once upon a time, in a world now impossible to remember and hard for some of us to imagine, the annual county fair was a huge event, which drew thousands of people to see the horse races and view the exhibits of livestock, fruit, flowers, crafts, and other products. Moreover, in the nineteenth century the fair was a profound expression of community in a county that prided itself on epitomizing the best in rural America, and the fairground also became the setting for some other important cultural events.

As local historian Alex Holmes pointed out many years ago, the first fair was held in 1855 "at the old McDonough College grounds," a half mile east of the square at Carroll and College Streets, and two years later it was moved to "Thompson Chandler's pasture west of Johnson Street and north of Adams Street." After the Civil War, in 1867, it was moved again, to a twenty-two-acre site south of Macomb, where the high school and armory are now located.

That more permanent location was "the fairground" for over fifty years. A half-mile racetrack and a grandstand immediately marked the facility, as well as a small frame exhibition building known as Floral Hall. The latter was never adequate for the exhibits or the crowds and was open to the weather on the sides, so in 1874 a new, much larger, and completely enclosed Floral Hall took its place. The nearby fenced-in "wagon yard" (parking lot) could hold well over five hundred vehicles.

The exhibits, especially flowers and needlework, were often described by the newspapers in glowing terms, but the biggest attraction was the horse

People assembled at a late nineteenth-century county fair, with the judges' stand and grandstand in the background.

racing. In the later nineteenth century, McDonough County was known for horse breeding, so trotting races were held every year for several decades. In 1929, long after the fairs had ceased, Vivian Brooking, who had left to settle in Nebraska during the 1880s, stopped to muse on the old fairground during a trip to Macomb, and he wrote this vivid recollection:

> *I visited the old fairground, and in fancy I could see the big crowd that always thronged Floral Hall and the grandstand when the races were on. The dance platform, and Dave Hampton between sets with his hamper of lemonade, saying, "Refresh your ladies." Old man Brady and Brose Updegraff strolling up and down the track with blankets on their arms.*

Uncle Viv Brooking and Dr. Blaisdell in the judges' stand. Andy Tatman walking up and down before the grandstand, with a ten-dollar bill between his fingers, offering to bet on his favorite. Winslow Taylor with a crowd around him, listening to his quips. [Trotting horse] *"Johnny Morgan" always getting the flag when he won, except the day when the track was muddy. Old "G.T. Pilot" getting half a quarter behind, and then lapping out the leaders. "Mollie Jones," the unbeatable mare at a mile...and many other famous racehorses.*

That was the life. Now the old fairground looks dilapidated and unused, but the memories of those days defy the ravages of time. They linger on, and no doubt will to the end.

His memoir reminds us that what was most important about the fairs, aside from the trotting races, was the intense social interaction.

Perhaps no aspect of the fairground had a greater mystique than the tall monument to the war horse and breeding stallion Chickamauga, which stood in the center of the track. I told his story many years ago, in *McDonough County Heritage*, but it is briefly this: Acquired in Tennessee during the Civil War by Colonel Louis H. Waters, who rode him through the Battle of Chickamauga and other engagements, the horse was later sold and did dray work in Macomb. But he was also raced at local fairs. He won, for example, the first trotting race held at the permanent fairground, in 1867, even though he was then ten years old. Eventually, Chickamauga was sold to a breeder outside of McDonough County, in about 1870, but he had already sired some winning trotters, and stories were also being told about the aging stallion's service in the war. So Chickamauga was sought, re-purchased in Iowa, and returned to Macomb in the summer of 1873. He became a celebrated county fair attraction, and owner A.V. Brooking promoted him as a stud horse—renaming his noted horse-breeding operation north of Macomb "Chickamauga Stock Farm." A newspaper article from about 1880 recalls the horse's final years and his monument:

> [Chickamauga] *was bought for $300 and brought back here* [in 1873], *and was met at the depot by the band. He was led through the principal streets of Macomb, headed by the band. He made several seasons here, but at last he got his leg broken and had to be shot. Many of the 84th* [Infantry Regiment] *boys followed the old hero's remains to their last resting place, where they were deposited beneath a green, growing oak on McDonough County's fairground, by the track where the hoofs of his descendants will be heard to clatter for generations to come. Now stands a stone monument, 16 feet high, over his grave, and inscribed on it: "Chickamauga. Bred by Rev. Talbert Fanning; sired by Vermont Boy; dam Mary, by Canada Chief; grandam Miss Foot, by Gray Eagle. Died July 2, 1878."*

The *Macomb Journal* printed a detailed account of his death, celebrating him as "the old hero of smoke and thunder, and blood and war—the old hero who, in a foreign land, without a name, without a pedigree, with scarcely a friend, arose by his own efforts from scrub obscurity to an equine prince." Some newspapers outside the county carried articles on the horse, and several years later, his story was also told in a national

W.O. Blaisdell, physician and horse breeder, who headed the Agricultural and Stock Association that developed the county fairs. He died in 1903.

racing magazine, *Spirit of the Turf*. Chickamauga had become a legend. No wonder his tall monument was an attraction at the fairground for several decades.

The burial ceremony for Chickamauga, with GAR members, was not the only Civil War–related event held at the fairground, for in 1879 and 1882 huge reunions of war veterans were centered there. In the second of those, for example, hundreds of men who had served in the Sixteenth, Seventy-eighth, and Eighty-fourth Infantry Regiments, and in others, tented there, held a meeting at Floral Hall, sang campaign songs like "Marching through Georgia," heard a patriotic address by Governor Oglesby, and even reenacted a battle "in the center of the track, while ten thousand spectators looked on." The event received wide publicity in the region.

Unfortunately, in the early twentieth century, attendance at the county fairs dwindled, partly because such committed leaders and horse breeders as Dr. W.O. Blaisdell and A.V. Brooking had passed away, and partly because horse breeding itself was declining—and with it, the interest in trotting races. The annual county fair finally ended in 1915, although it was revived a couple of times during the century.

The last great cultural event held at the old fairground was the huge "Community Pageant" developed in late May 1924. Perhaps the key figure behind the event was Western's early historian James Burns, who wrote the script for the production, which featured an episode about the Indians, a series of pioneer events set in the 1820s, a reconstruction of Lincoln's 1860 campaign as experienced in Macomb, a dramatic conflict over the local Underground Railroad, and the response of local people to the coming of the Civil War. The pageant was staged in front of the grandstand, and it involved more than three hundred local people in the various historical roles and as dancers. The Macomb Band provided the music. Performed twice, on May 29 and 30, the pageant drew large, appreciative crowds.

Perhaps the most significant thing about the complex production was the town's interest in promoting community life by appreciating local heritage. As the *Macomb Journal* pointed out, "All ages join hands and hearts in this wonderful story…. A glorious drama, and true to life. The real yesterdays of real people—our forefathers, who transformed the wild hunting ground of the Redman into this beautiful site, and made possible the building of our prosperous city. It is a story worth the telling."

At that time, a sense of local heritage was still common in Macomb and McDonough County, as it had been since the post–Civil War years, but times were rapidly changing. The last of the pioneers were dying, and the Depression and World War II would soon bring other priorities. Once a symbol of community life in the past, the old fairground was sold to the Board of Education in 1931 for an athletic complex, which was not developed until the 1940s. However, the structures were dismantled then, at the outset of the Depression. As local historian Kathy Nichols has pointed out in a recent article, "Today, all that remains from the fairground is the original ticket-and-entry gate, located in a private yard on Grant Street."

And no one knows what happened to the monument for Chickamauga, which was also, as it turned out, a monument to horse breeding and trotting races, Civil War memories, and fairground excitement—the times that were in nineteenth-century McDonough County.

Colchester's Pleasant Valley—and Ragtown

Long before Colchester was established, there was a north–south trail seven miles west of Macomb passing through the timber, brush, and prairie grass. About one mile north of where the coal mining town would later be platted, that old trail (now county road 500 East) led down between steep bluffs to a ford at Crooked Creek, set in a lovely dale of oak and hickory trees.

The vast open land to the north, in Hire Township, was called "the North Prairie." The smaller section of open land to the south, in Tennessee Township, was called "the South Prairie." Lying in between, and connecting them, the ford in the valley was an ideal place for a mill, so a man named Jacob Emerick built one there in 1838, with the help of nearby farmers. That frontier business venture eventually paved the way for a notable recreation area in what came to be called Pleasant Valley, and the road leading into that area from the north also became the main street of a rural neighborhood called Ragtown.

The mill changed hands a number of times during the nineteenth century. Emerick soon sold it to Allen Key, who sold it to partners named Reuben Harrington and John Proctor, who in turn sold it to Cornelius Carmack and his son. The Carmacks ran it for many years and then sold it before the Civil War to John and Newman Foster, father and son, who ran it until 1871. Then they sold it to John (Jake) Myers, who was the final owner of the mill, which ceased operation in the early 1890s. The mill lasted for more than fifty years, which was far longer than most of the pioneer water mills in McDonough County.

By mid-century, it was known as Pleasant Valley Mill. The big frame building was three stories high and had an extension on one side to create living quarters for the miller's family. In the early days, it was the largest building for many miles, and it was a natural gathering place for the pioneers, where "neighbors" who lived miles apart could discuss crops, livestock, and politics while waiting for their grain to be ground.

After local coal mining began and the railroad went through in the 1850s, Argyle Hollow (where the state park is today) had many drift mines. When Colchester developed south of the creek, as the nearby trading point, people traveled to and from there by way of the old Pleasant Valley road.

After the Civil War, the Pleasant Valley Mill area became a popular place to both fish and picnic. It was a kind of unofficial park. According to local resident Janie Irish, in about 1870 "a wooden dam was built nearby…to accumulate water for use by the steam engines, to power the trains." The dammed-up water was pumped to the tower in Colchester. Of course, the presence of the dam soon made that a noted fishing spot on Crooked Creek, which led to picnics as well. A serio-comic article entitled "Picnicking," in the 1888 *Colchester Independent*, reveals the experiences and activities that made the mill site a popular place:

> *The vicinity of the Pleasant Valley Mill continues to be a popular fishing and picnic resort. Every week during the picnic season parties from far and near go there to enjoy the cool shade and velvety wild lawn, the pure air, the fragrance of flowers, the singing birds and rippling waters, the fishless angling, the ants, the mosquitoes, the falls in the creek (if it don't rain), the muddying of clothes and getting them befloured at the old mill, the getting scared at frightened snakes and kind-hearted cows, the wearisomeness of climbing the nearby bluffs…all necessary to the enjoyment and success of a day's outing. It was a merry company of picnickers that came in sixteen buggies from the country in the vicinities of Blandinsville and Sciota on Saturday—all young folks.*

Because the mill road made for easy access to the water, the area was also used during the summer for baptisms by some religious denominations, and of course, boys from the nearby Ragtown neighborhood, and from Colchester in general, often swam there as well. At the century's end, the old mill was such a popular place that it was featured on a local postcard. By then, it had become a symbol of pioneer days.

On the left is the Pleasant Valley Mill, circa 1900. At the right is the CB&Q pumping station and the dam.

A baptism in Crooked Creek, near the Pleasant Valley Mill, in the late nineteenth century.

Although the picturesque, abandoned mill collapsed in 1910 and was afterward disposed of, seven years later a group of Colchester businessmen formed the Pleasant Valley Club, which proceeded "to stock the creek with fish" and turn the area into "a park or pleasure resort." Started with seventeen families, the club grew rapidly and had two hundred member families by the end of the decade.

Picnic tables were set up, and a clubhouse with dressing rooms was built on the north side of the creek. People came to swim, fish, and boat on the water above the little dam. The Pleasant Valley Club operated until sometime in the 1930s, and it was replaced, in a sense, by the coming of Spring Lake Park, northwest of Macomb, in the later 1920s—which offered better fishing and boating, as well as swimming and picnicking—and by the development of Lake Argyle State Park in the 1940s.

While all that was going on, over several generations, the area up the hill (to the north) from Pleasant Valley developed into the Ragtown neighborhood. The residents were coal-mining families. The men and boys there worked in drift mines near the creek and to the west, in a place called Welch's Hollow. Supposedly, the name of their rural hamlet arose from the use of rags by local residents to cover holes in broken windows—or because the neighborhood children wore patches on their clothes. But both of those explanations are folklore. Most coal-mining families elsewhere were equally poor.

Years ago, I interviewed the oldest person in Ragtown, a woman named Opal Burton, who was then in her early nineties, and she told me that shortly after she and her husband came there in 1922, she heard from an old woman in the Kipling family that before the Civil War some pioneer families with covered wagons had gathered at that place for several weeks before leaving for the West. Because of the cloth tops of those assembled wagons, the area became known as Ragtown. After they left, the colorful name stuck.

William Kipling and his family were, in fact, among the earliest residents of the Ragtown area. An 1883 article in the *Colchester Independent* mentions the effort of his sons to get ahead through coal mining:

> *Four brothers, William, John, Thomas, and Albert, sons of William Kipling, have bought 26 acres of first class coal land lying in the vicinity of "Rag Town," from Jefferson Welch. Price: $50 per acre. The buyers are young men, who have been working for years in the mines and who, by saving their money, are now enabled to go into the coal business for themselves.*

Ragtown had a school, located at what is now the corner of county roads 500 East and 1150 North. Thirty years ago, retired teacher and administrator Albert Burgard recalled his experience teaching there in the 1920s. He told me that many schoolboys also worked part time in the mines. They would help to dig a load of coal in the morning and then come to school. Held back by their work experience, many of the eighth-grade boys were in their middle teens. Yet by then, the coal-mining era in Colchester was passing away.

Burgard also recalled the Ragtown Store from his childhood. It was a small frame building across the road, to the east, from the school. In the spring during the nineteenth century, when Crooked Creek had overflowed its banks, people from the North Prairie couldn't get to Colchester, so they shopped in Ragtown—or so he had been told.

Old-time auctioneer Hughey Martin, who grew up in the nearby Argyle Hollow area, told me that there was a strong but informal sense of community in Ragtown—among the Bunts, Burtons, Fentems, Kiplings, Websters, and other families. They even had a sort of unofficial mayor or spokesman. One short article I later found in the 1927 *Colchester Independent* explained the hamlet's curious leadership tradition:

> *It is not necessary for Ragtown to go to the expense of holding an election, as all offices are filled by appointment. According to a time-honored custom, the last man to move into this little settlement, which is located a short distance north of here, is given the honor of being the mayor. At present Charles Carmack is the chief executive, and according to his friends, he will make a very able official.*

Of course, the Ragtown school closed with the coming of consolidation, and now nothing remains to mark the old coal-mining hamlet, which once had a dozen small, white frame houses. Just to the south, the Pleasant Valley Mill has been gone for a century, and the later recreation facilities have been long torn down or removed. The old road winding down from the Ragtown corner to the mill grounds, where pioneers once forded the river, leads nowhere now—except into a heavily forested, river-bluff terrain, where a sign says, at the edge of the valley, "Road Closed."

Vishnu Springs: Resort Town and Wildlife Sanctuary

The struggle to found viable communities in McDonough County began in 1826 at Carter's Settlement, near present-day Industry. It ended more than sixty years later at Vishnu Springs, which has been a ghost town for most of a century. No village in the county's history began with greater publicity or generated more local talk, but none was more surely doomed to failure. And mingled with the fate of the community was the violent death of the man who founded it, Darius Hicks.

The first person to promote the place where Vishnu Springs would be located was Dr. John W. Aiken. Born in Ohio in 1836, he came to the village of Tennessee in 1865 to practice medicine. For the rest of the century, he was the only physician in that tiny community. By the 1870s, the little fountain of water in the valley northwest of town was known as Tennessee Springs. The community held an annual picnic there for many years. In September 1883, a crowd of seven hundred to one thousand people listened to the Macomb Band and heard speeches by politician William H. Neece, newspaperman B.R. Hampton, and others.

Earlier that year, Dr. Aiken had leased the twenty acres around Tennessee Springs from the county's wealthiest farmer, Ebenezer Hicks, so that he could have the water tested for medicinal qualities and consider establishing a resort. After the analysis was made at Rush Medical College in Chicago, he changed the name to Vishnu Medical Springs and began to promote his business venture. Vishnu is the second member of the Hindu trinity, in which God manifests Himself as the Preserver of living things. Hence, with that name, the doctor was trying to associate his "medical springs" with health and longevity.

Dr. Aiken subscribed to the common notion that mineral water had specific health benefits, and he started using the Vishnu Springs water in treating his patients. An early advertisement in the *Colchester Independent* is full of curative claims:

> *These waters are proving very valuable in gouty or uric acid diathesis, inflammation of the bladder and kidneys, Bright's disease, disorder of the stomach and nervous system, general debility, and diseases peculiar to women. Hundreds visit the springs every day. The water retains its properties when shipped. For information or water, which will be delivered on* [railroad] *cars in jugs from Tennessee for 25 cents per gal., address Dr. Aiken & Co., Tennessee, Ill.*

When Ebenezer Hicks died in June 1886, his wife and three children shared an estate worth half a million dollars, and it was his son Darius, then thirty-six years old, who fell heir to Vishnu Springs. He continued the lease with Aiken but began to plan the development of a community.

Since Vishnu was conceptualized as a health resort, Hicks had to build a hotel. He went into partnership with John Mourning, who owned a nearby stone quarry, and by May 1889 a twenty-six- by forty-foot building was being erected near the spring. Named the Capitol Hotel, the three-story frame structure, with twenty-four guest rooms and a banquet room, was finished in September and cost over $2,500.

During that first summer, Hicks began to publicize the community. His most effective effort was the scheduling of a Holiness Movement camp meeting there, which drew two to three thousand people. Individuals began buying lots, and by October 1889, Vishnu Springs had its first settler, Andrew Ruddle, who built a rough board shanty not far from the hotel. In the winter of 1890, David Reece opened the first store.

By the following spring, 1890, the community had two more stores, a restaurant (in the hotel), a livery barn, and a photo gallery. Hicks and Mourning organized the Vishnu Transfer Line, which made trips from Colchester to the new resort area, especially on weekends. As W.W. Vose reported in early June for the *Macomb Journal*, "For 75 cents the passenger is transported to the Springs, gets dinner at the new hotel, and is brought back."

Although the Colchester paper reported that "Vishnu is on the boom," there was also trouble at the springs. Hicks evidently did not get along with

The Capitol Hotel at Vishnu Springs was built in 1889. This gathering marked the opening of it.

co-developer Charles K. Way, and there was talk of dividing the community into two parts. Way eventually developed land southeast of the hotel.

Also, the resort became known for the sale and consumption of illegal alcohol—or "bootleg whisky," as the newspaper called it—and the drinking led to occasional fights. In the fall of 1890, for example, Andrew Ruddle stabbed restaurant proprietor John Mourning and was subsequently arrested. Some months before that, Hicks had bought Mourning's interest in the hotel so he could be more firmly in charge.

Hicks did continue to develop the resort and community. A new organ was installed in the hotel parlor, and the lawn soon had swings, hammocks, croquet grounds, a picnic area, and a pond (called Lake Vishnu) stocked with goldfish. Hicks also built a racetrack and established a park with a horse-drawn merry-go-round. All of that was not in the valley but on a nearby hill. He promoted or arranged cultural activities as well, including Fourth of July celebrations, dances, and band concerts. He organized a literary society and built a schoolhouse for his new community, too.

In spite of his efforts during the early 1890s, Vishnu Springs never had more than twelve or fifteen small homes, and of course, the hotel was not active in cold weather. The village failed to develop a sound economic base—which is not surprising for an isolated resort community with no railroad connections. However, Vishnu Springs did have a post office for several years, starting in 1896. Hicks moved to the community from his nearby farm and was postmaster for a couple of years.

If the struggle of Darius Hicks to found a viable community was frustrating, his personal life was characterized by even greater problems. Married in 1874, he was already divorced from his first wife, Ella, who took their three daughters to Indiana, before he started developing Vishnu Springs. In 1889, he was married for a second time, to Hattie Rush of Missouri, who had evidently come to the springs for health reasons. She too had been married before and had children of her own, including a twelve-year-old daughter named Maud. Unfortunately, Hattie suffered from a variety of illnesses, including Bright's disease, heart trouble, and dropsy—and the water didn't help. She died in 1896, at the age of forty.

Whether the second marriage of Darius Hicks was happier than the first one is unknown, but in the following year, he did something that scandalized many of his contemporaries: he married his stepdaughter. Maud became the third Mrs. Hicks in September 1897 in a private, civil ceremony at the McDonough County Courthouse. She was twenty years old, and he was forty-seven.

Although the marriage was not actually incestuous, it had similar psychological ramifications, and most people viewed it as improper. Probably for that reason, Hicks moved away from the Vishnu Springs area, to a farm north of Blandinsville. Of course, he became much less involved with his resort community.

Maud Hicks gave birth to a son in 1898 and a daughter in 1901. But two years later, she died in childbirth, at the age of twenty-six. The infant died also.

Hicks soon hired a housekeeper named Nellie Darrah, a widow, who was especially needed to help care for his two small children. In the years that followed, she became a mother figure for them. She also became sexually involved with Hicks. By the winter of 1908, Mrs. Darrah was pregnant. Hicks evidently refused to marry her, and she subsequently got an abortion in LaHarpe. But the procedure, done that spring, did not go well, and she had to be hospitalized.

When Mrs. Darrah threatened to publicize the whole matter, Hicks got out his .32-caliber rifle and shot himself in the head on June 15. According to the *Macomb Journal*, he left a note "stating that he committed the deed because he was in trouble with a woman; that the same was sure to come out to the public, and that he could not live and face his children after the exposure." A subsequent article identified the woman as Nellie Darrah and referred to the "criminal operation" that led to her illness.

The death of Darius Hicks was a significant blow to the struggling community of Vishnu Springs, for he had continued to be involved in the town's business after moving to Blandinsville. There was no one else with as much money or as great a personal interest in the village. It went into permanent decline, while stories circulated about illicit gambling and drinking there.

By the 1920s, Vishnu Springs was a legend-haunted ghost town. In 1935, nature lover Ira Post bought the long unused hotel and 220 acres. His daughter, Betty Post Cutler, who lived to be 104, later told me that he hired carpenter Lon Cale to restore the building and then Cale lived in it as a caretaker. Post and his wife Reatha also used it as a summer home, living on the second floor. In the late 1930s, Post put up a sign inviting visitors to use his private park, where they could "drink of the spring water, and enjoy nature," asking only that people "leave the flowers, ferns, rocks, trees, birds, and wildlife just as it is." And according to Mrs. Cutler, "visitors again came by the hundreds."

In 1951, Ira Post died. After years of disuse, the property was rented by Alfred White and Albert Simmons in the late 1960s, and they opened a weekend restaurant at the hotel, which closed after several years. In the 1970s and early 1980s, some Western Illinois University students rented the hotel, which was a kind of very-far-off-campus housing, but since then it has been unoccupied. In 2003, the Posts' granddaughter, Olga Kay Kennedy, donated the property that had been Vishnu Springs to WIU, and it is now known as the Ira and Reatha T. Post Wildlife Sanctuary. Funds are being sought to restore the hotel and develop the property, chiefly for use by science students. A Macomb-area group, the Friends of Vishnu, is working to clean up the grounds and promote restoration of the old hotel. Through them, the old ghost town has a website, complete with photographs: www.vishnusprings.org.

No other vanished community or rural neighborhood in McDonough County has anywhere near the mystique about it, or public interest in it, that Vishnu Springs has. And thanks to the donor and the university, the site also has a future—and an important purpose.

Memories and Ghost Stories of Scott's Church and Cemetery

One of the most remote and lovely places in McDonough County is the old Scott's neighborhood in Bethel Township, some seventeen miles south of Macomb. It is not a ghost town because it never was a village; but an isolated church, with a cemetery, has stood there for generations. In more ways than one, it is a "ghost neighborhood."

A sense of distinctive place began with pioneer settlers—the Scotts, the Holtons, the Hendricksons, and others—who established a cemetery on a beautiful hill in 1836 and, five years later, built a log church there too. When that pioneer church burned down at the close of the Civil War, the families in that rural neighborhood built a frame one, and that, in turn, was superseded by the 1896 church that still stands on the hill, just south of the cemetery.

For many years, the church bell could be heard across the fields and through the forests every Sunday morning. However, after the belfry was struck by lightning in 1927, the bell was removed for a time. That wooden tower was eventually rebuilt, but decades later the church roof leaked, so the belfry was dismantled permanently in about 1960, and the old bell was mounted in a frame on the front lawn.

More than a place of worship, Scott's Church was also a community center where rural people gathered "to sing, to pray, to grieve, to hope, to eat with friends, and to enjoy life more fully," as local historian Charles Stump put it. But as the rural population declined in the twentieth century, church attendance dwindled, and the consolidation of rural schools—including nearby Buncombe and Shanghai—during the 1940s eroded the sense of

A contemporary photograph of Scott's Church, with the bell placed in a frame on the lawn, and the cemetery to the north of it.

neighborhood identity that had marked the area for over a century. In the 1950s, only occasional services were held at the church, but Sunday school continued there for many years. Now the building is abandoned, and it symbolizes a bygone era, an increasingly unremembered time.

But it happens that the most prominent McDonough County writer of the early twentieth century spent some of his boyhood years in that rural neighborhood. Jay House was born on a farm half a mile east of the church, in the old Buncombe School District of Lamoine Township, in 1870. When he was ten, his family moved to Kansas, where the boy learned the printing trade. Despite his limited, country school education, he eventually edited the *Topeka Daily Capital* and became, in fact, the mayor of Topeka during World War I. In 1919, he joined the staff of the *Philadelphia Ledger*, where he continued his daily column, "On Second Thought." Starting in the 1920s, he also wrote many articles for the *Saturday Evening Post*, including two that reflect his family's experience in McDonough County. By then he was a nationally known figure. His last article for the *Post*, the autobiographical "Saga of a Farm Family," appeared just after his death in 1936.

At the close of the 1920s, House made a trip to McDonough County to visit a few remaining relatives and childhood acquaintances, and that visit prompted two brief memoirs that appeared in the *Philadelphia Ledger* and were reprinted in the *Macomb Journal*. The first is about family activities in the 1880s, including a trip by wagon over muddy roads to see a circus parade in Macomb.

The other article, titled "The Old, Old Neighborhood," is more fascinating—a memoir of the rural community that centered on Scott's Church. House vividly recalls the earlier, smaller church building and the strict Methodist congregation that gathered there to battle against the devil:

> *The old place…was a militant fortress of religion, which dared the devil to do his worst and fought him at every turn. It was a low building, without architectural grace or dignity. It had no bell or belfry, and in winter cold winds swept the open recesses underneath and penetrated the cracks in the floor. Two great stoves, stacked with wood, burned red hot in winter. Those near to them roasted, and the teeth of those more distant chattered from the cold….*
>
> *Married men sat on one side of the church, married women on the other. Boys and girls who were "going together" sat in the middle row of seats. The seats were straight-backed, hard and uncomfortable. In the corner to the left of the pulpit sat the militant sisters, the shouting cohorts of the Lord. In the corner to the right sat the militant men, who lifted up their voices in praise and thanksgiving. They had church then—bless you, yes—twice every Sunday…. And every winter there were weeks of revival services, in which many sinners were reclaimed.*

Church in the old Scott's neighborhood, in those days, was clearly a dead-serious business, much like it had been for the Puritans in old New England.

House also recalls some of the ghost stories associated with the old church and burying ground, for it might be expected that people so focused on sin and escaping the snares of the devil were filled with barely repressed anxieties. One tale centers on a frightening confrontation with a huge man in black:

> *There was the Pressley Hobbs ghost. Pressley, returning home from a day's labor in the fields, had occasion to walk past Scott's Church, at night. Just below the crest of the hill a very tall man, clad in robes of black, suddenly confronted him. He* [Pressley] *turned away, heading down the hill, but the man again confronted him. Again* [Pressley] *turned toward the crest, and*

> *there again was the tall man in the middle of the road. Thereupon, Pressley climbed the fence and ran himself sick, across the adjacent dark field.*

Of course, that spooky tale is psychologically suggestive. What was Pressley Hobbs trying to avoid? His sense of guilt? His fear of death? Or simply the devil, waiting for him in the dark? Perhaps only in a remote, deeply religious place would such an experience or a story arise.

House also recalls a tale that may have its origin in the giant-wolf-in-the-woods stories that still circulated in a half-forested county that had not completely eliminated those frightening predators:

> *Daniel Hance had been* [to see] *the doctor and was returning home. He was on horseback, at dusk. At the cemetery, an enormous dog, three or four times as large as any dog he had ever seen, began running beside him, keeping just at the horse's withers. Daniel drove his horse to its ultimate in speed, but the great dog kept easily running alongside. After awhile, he out-distanced it, but Daniel was a pretty scared man by the time he returned home.*

House also remembers hearing of the tragic death, before his time, of a relative in his mother's family—a death that haunted the minds of local residents: "And there was also the Jake Wier ghost. Jake's team had run away, and he had been thrown from his wagon and killed at the corner just south of the church. For years thereafter, people passing the cemetery heard the clatter of hoofs, the rattle of a wagon, and other reverberations of that fatal runaway."

House recalled those stories about "the ghosts of Scott's Church" because they once had a powerful impact on him. As he remarks in his 1929 article:

> *The road leading up the hill past the cemetery and to the church was ghost country, nothing less. Most people pretended not to believe in ghosts, but everybody talked about them. I used to sit around the listen and grow terror-stricken. I wouldn't have passed Scott's Church Cemetery alone after nightfall for all the wealth of the Indies. And I don't know whether I'd do it yet.*

His comments also remind us that stories embedded in the culture of a particular place—even ghost stories—once bound local residents to their home area by giving them a sense of shared experience. Because those stories circulated orally, the vast majority of them have been lost. That we have even a few from the "ghost country" of Scott's neighborhood resulted from the improbable circumstance that a noted American writer, with a long memory, emerged from that remote township of McDonough County.

The Gooseneck Neighborhood and Its Famous Ghost

The most widely discussed Macomb-area phenomenon of the early twentieth century was the Gooseneck Ghost, a mysterious apparition that horrified, intrigued, and entertained the local populace but was never satisfactorily explained. It also made the rural neighborhood where it appeared a legendary place.

The ghost began to appear in early January 1908. Its haunt was the Gooseneck neighborhood, between two and three miles west of Macomb, located along the railroad tracks and, later, Route 136. That well-known rural area, where the road curved like a gooseneck, was centered on a small, white-frame schoolhouse that had been there for several decades. According to an initial report by the *Macomb Journal*,

> *The ghost has appeared on a number of occasions and has been seen by quite a few of the farmers. Its haunt is along the railroad, and it seems to come as far east as the Taylor lane, which is about two miles west of this city, leading from the Colchester road, and wanders up and down the track and over into the fields. It appears in the form of a bright light….*
>
> *Saturday night, as Joe Morton and his boy were going home, the ghost appeared and flashed his light directly into the faces of Mr. Morton and son. The team* [of horses], *which is usually staid and quiet, was afraid of the supernatural and started to run…. William Taylor declares that the ghost chased him, and he did a sprint of two hundred yards at a gait* [faster than] *a jackrabbit at full speed…. Charles Culp, Thomas Beverly, and others have also seen the ghost.*

The newspaper article created much anxiety and set off a wave of speculation about the ghost. Anybody unusual or anything strange in the Gooseneck area was connected with the apparition. The *Journal* soon reported the following incident: "The [railroad] section men, who belong to the Colchester [work] gang, report seeing a mysterious stranger in that vicinity at different times. Monday, when they were on their handcar, they saw the man, and as they approached, he stepped from the railroad and disappeared."

The very next night, "the Ogden boys heard a sound like a woman's scream" coming across the fields, and the county sheriff was called to investigate—but found nothing. To many local residents, the ghost had become something fearful and sinister.

Groups of men and boys began organizing after dark to hunt for the ghost. Some of them were armed. Anyone they encountered was stopped and questioned, which gave rise to such incidents as the following: "Steve Willey was walking to Colchester last night and was stopped by some of the neighbors and accused of being the ghost, which he denied."

Others began to offer explanations for the mysterious light. Most of them were very unlikely, but some, like the following one, were reported in the newspaper: "Lester Butterfield says he can explain the lights that have created the ghost west of this city. He claims that his boys and the Fugate boys get over in the fields and run at each other with lighted cornstalks. The fire flies from the end of the burning stalks like a skyrocket." The boys quit lighting cornstalks, but the ghost sightings continued.

By late January, various local residents had seen the ghost near an old elm tree, and it was apparent that folkloric exaggeration had begun to color accounts of the apparition:

> *The Gooseneck ghost has been seen again, and it ran after William Taylor until he fell exhausted in an effort to get into the house. The ghost seems to have taken up its habitation in or near a large elm tree near the* [railroad] *crossing at Til Bowen's and Arthur Clayton's. Lou Bowen saw it Monday night at the elm tree, and saw it go up the tree, where it apparently disappeared. It ran up like a flash. Ed and Charles Culp also saw it in the tree one night recently, and it suddenly disappeared, only to reappear a quarter of a mile away almost instantly. They say the light is brighter than the searchlight on a locomotive.*

Teacher Maud Hodges and her students at the Gooseneck School in 1913. Some of them had surely seen the famous ghost.

Others claimed that the light had a human face or would suddenly change into the image of a fire-breathing dragon. No wonder nearby newspapers began reprinting the *Journal*'s Gooseneck Ghost articles.

In the late spring of 1908, a group of Western Illinois State Normal professors went to the Gooseneck area to investigate. After seeing the ghost, they "explained that it was a case of 'will-o-the-wisp,' or 'Jack-o-lanterns,' as [marsh gas is] commonly called." However, since most of the sightings had taken place in January, when the temperature was well below freezing, their marsh gas theory was not very convincing.

Naturally, some people thought that the light was truly a ghost. Among them was Farnum B. Camp, who asserted that the Gooseneck area had been the scene of six or seven violent deaths: "Four men were killed on a railroad track by being run over by the train; also, two track layers were murdered by fellow workmen when the railroad was in the course of construction back in the 1850s." Others recalled that an old man had hanged himself in the big elm tree some years ago. So, to some folks, there was more than one ghost, and the lights were simply the spirits of the dead, lingering near the locations where they had been killed.

Many others in the Macomb area viewed the Gooseneck Ghost (or Ghosts) less seriously. In late June, a group of young adults called the Moonlighters organized an ice cream supper to be held at a grove in the Gooseneck neighborhood, for the purpose of capturing the ghost. Some three hundred people came, including a number of children who attended the Gooseneck School. Among them was Lora Lemmer, who was then thirteen, and whose family had already seen the ghost several times. Decades later, she recalled the event:

> *That night there were so many horses and buggies going to the grove that the road dust hung in the air, almost like a fog, but that didn't quell the spirits of the young folks that night. They were out on a ghost hunt.... We mingled with the crowd, ate all the ice cream we could hold, and had a grand time in general.*
>
> *About nine o'clock a shout went up: "There it is! There it is!" And sure enough, a little ball of light was slowly rising over the railroad tracks way down in the west. It grew larger as it sailed slowly down the tracks toward the picnic grove—and then just before it reached* [us], *it disappeared.*

About two weeks later, the *Journal* reported that a few Macomb residents had captured the ghost. It proved to be "a Japanese lantern which was attached to the tail of a kite." However, while the kite was recovered, the person who flew it was not. For many local residents, that was sufficient explanation for the Gooseneck Ghost. But others were skeptical. Who would go out on windy, near-zero January nights to fly a kite for any reason? And what about those who were chased by the ghost, or who saw it at the old elm tree, or who saw faces in the light? The kite-and-lantern explanation seemed plausible for the recent sightings, at the ice cream supper and perhaps elsewhere in the summer, but not for the ghost of the previous winter. Even the *Macomb Journal* reporter suggested that "some jokers fixed up a burlesque and planned that it should be captured, to ridicule the [all-too-seriously discussed] mystery of the strange lights."

Whatever the case, the Gooseneck Ghost did not appear anymore that year. But three years later, in the spring of 1911, the mysterious light was seen again, and it was the talk of the neighborhood. And toward the end of 1912, it appeared once more, prompting the Macomb newspaper to report that "the celebrated ghost is again on a rampage." And in February 1915, three men saw the ghost coming "from the direction of the schoolhouse, and [moving] south, sometimes near the ground and other times high up in the air, until it reached the railroad track at the exact spot where a man by the name of Rousch was killed by a train a number of years ago." Whatever the ghost was, it seemed to know about past deaths in the neighborhood. And, of course, there were surely other sightings of the ghost that went unreported in the newspaper.

So the strange phenomenon remained a mystery—at least, to many people. But it gave a lasting, if spooky, identity to the now vanished rural community centered on a white-frame country school where the kids of that era shared countless stories about the local apparition. And still, a century later, no one has heard of the Gooseneck neighborhood west of Macomb who has not also heard of the ghost.

Western's Nature Area, the Ravine, and Its Theater

In 1902, Western Illinois State Normal School opened on a hill northwest of the Macomb square, and as the campus developed, with a lawn and flowerbeds, trees, and shrubs, the wooded ravine just to the east of the huge building was soon regarded by students and teachers as a lovely place to stroll. As one alumna put it, looking back over half a century, "The ravine was wild and woodsy in those days, with paths winding through it that afforded many happy meanderings, when one had the time." Within a few years, the ravine became a noted nature spot, a sort of institutional park where Western groups held activities, classes posed for photographs, and eventually the school operated a summer theater. Those days are now long past, but since the ravine did have so many public functions, its remarkable history can be recovered in some detail.

Because a small, sluggish stream—often called Normal Creek—flowed through the ravine, two rustic log bridges were constructed in about 1906. One was fairly close to Adams Street, just down from where Lincoln Hall is today, and the other, longer one was farther north, down the hill from where Morgan Gym was later constructed. The idea for the two bridges probably came from Samuel Hursh, the first English professor and the acting president during 1905–1906.

Even before he became an administrator, Hursh was noted for his leadership in campus beautification, and he had also arranged for additional trees to be planted in the ravine. His house stood across West Adams Street, facing the ravine, and he loved to walk through the little wooded valley. A believer in

By the 1940s, the early paths in the ravine had become cement sidewalks and the long, wooden bridge had been replaced with a stone one. In the distance is the Ravine Theater.

the positive spiritual impact of nature, he became noted for leading nature excursions on campus—excursions that always included the ravine. It is not surprising that when he retired in 1925, July 15 was designated as "Hursh Day" at Western, and alumni, faculty, and townspeople who had known him since 1902 assembled in the ravine to pay tribute to him.

Photographic postcards of the beloved nature area became popular during the Bayliss administration (1906–1911), as did class photographs taken at one of the rustic bridges. Some accounts of student gatherings in the ravine have survived, and among them is this item from the 1911 *Sequel*, which reveals the deep sense of community that prevailed at Western when there were only a few hundred students:

> *It was during the Summer School* [July 2, 1910] *that the class of 1911 gathered to bid farewell to a departing senior and to welcome new members with a moonlight picnic in the Normal ravine.... All having arrived at the best place, we made a fire and spread the table. Soon all was ready, and we sat down to a delicious repast, consisting of sandwiches, salads, pickles, fruit, cake, ice cream, and coffee. The "toasts" consisted of ghost stories told by each member. After the table was cleared away, we spent the evening in sports and games of different kinds. We danced an Indian war dance around the fire.*

The summer of 1911 marked the start of the Ravine Theater, which made the nature area well known in McDonough County. The first performances there were given on June 30 and July 1 by a traveling Shakespearean troupe called the Coburn Players, headed by veteran actor Charles Coburn. They performed *Much Ado about Nothing* and *Macbeth*, as well as a non-Shakespearean comedy called *The Canterbury Pilgrims*, based on Chaucer's famous tales.

Faculty members and townspeople were very pleased, so Western trustee John M. Keefer—who was then mayor of Macomb—led the Board of Trustees in providing funds to landscape the area and create cement tiers on which folding chairs could be placed. The theater was completed in early July 1913, when the Coburn players returned to perform three other Shakespearean plays.

The first student production in the ravine was *The Pied Piper of Hamelin.* It was presented on May 16, 1913, by the training school students as part of that year's Field Day (or outdoor activity) program. Some four hundred youngsters, all in costume, participated in the production, delighting their parents and others who sat in folding chairs or on the hillside behind them. Significantly, it was a play about community and the need for appreciation of both children and nature. The director was Nina Lamkin, Western's first real physical education specialist, who had developed the annual Field Day program.

In 1918, the Ravine Theater was also the venue for *The Pageant of Illinois*, a production commemorating the state's centennial, which featured such

Western training school students acting in *The Pied Piper of Hamelin* in 1913 at the Ravine Theater.

historical figures as Marquette and Joliet, LaSalle, and George Rogers Clark. The author and general director was Eloise Ramsey, a Western English teacher, but it was a group project that involved teachers of dancing and music as well. Hundreds of people attended the pageant, which reflected a communal appreciation for Illinois history that would eventually fade.

The most acclaimed production ever staged at the Ravine Theater, however, was another historical pageant, presented during the 1927 Homecoming, which marked the twenty-fifth anniversary of Western. Some 200 students performed in the massive work, which presented allegorical figures like History, the Spirit of Western, and Prophecy, as well as scenes from the past, such as "The Founding of Western" and "Western in the World War." Some 1,500 people watched the elaborate production, which also featured music by the college's orchestra, band, and glee clubs.

That commemorative production was developed by a faculty committee chaired by drama teacher Harold Schory, and it led to annual college plays, which he directed, starting in 1929. As Schory recalled at his retirement in 1960, "The area was treated to kill mosquitoes, lights would be placed in the wings, and footlights and spotlights would be set up. At 8 p.m. the actors, all in costume, would march down to the ravine from Sherman Hall. Usually between five hundred and eight hundred spectators would be present." Some of the plays were by Shakespeare, but others were performed too, including one written by Schory. Under his leadership, the outdoor theater eventually achieved a certain notoriety in the Midwest.

The Ravine Theater stopped having productions during World War II, was revived again from 1952 to 1954 for English Club plays directed by Merle Lundvall, ceased operating again for several years, and was revived for the last time in 1962 by Ronald Gee and Alfred Brooks of the Speech and Drama Department, who directed productions of *Room Service*, *Rashomon*, *Arms and the Man*, and *Alice in Wonderland*.

By that time, however, workmen were already beginning to change the ravine, for Lincoln and Washington Halls (twin fourteen-story dormitories) were going up and would open in 1963, and there was a married-student housing complex (East Village) planned for across the old creek. It opened in 1966. Over several years, many trees and shrubs were eliminated, and in 1967, storm tile was installed to contain the flowing stream, which had become polluted as the northwest part of Macomb developed. Final grading and seeding of the land to cover the storm tile and the exposed sewage pipes for the buildings was done in 1973, and then the "wild and woodsy" old ravine was completely gone, replaced by a sloping campus lawn.

In a 1962 article, a *Western Courier* editor wrote a requiem for the ravine, as the construction work was starting that would slowly destroy it. He or she had been around long enough to know what the university was losing, and expressed, for thousands of people, the closing of a memorable era: "The roar of tractors and the crash of trees have taken the place of students lounging in the ravine…. The scenic spot is now being cleared. Time has finally run out for the ravine, as we once knew it." The author then recalled the beautiful trees, the wandering brook, the old stone bridge (which had replaced the large wooden one), the winding paths, and the outdoor stage—and concluded that "the ravine glorified the campus."

Now the Ravine Theater is virtually the only recognizable feature of the little valley that was once the beloved campus nature area. Most students who attend Western today never even see that cement-tiered amphitheater, hidden down below the new Grote Hall and surrounded by overgrown trees and shrubs, like the ruins of an ancient temple. But to alumni and local residents with long memories, it symbolizes a vanished time when the university was still a normal school and teachers' college, characterized by a profound sense of common experience.

The Wilds of Crooked Creek

In nineteenth-century McDonough County, the Lamoine River—then called Crooked Creek—was not just an obstacle to travel and a source of water power for mills; it was also the locus of many hunting adventures and other wildlife encounters and, hence, the setting for countless stories. That expanse of forest and flowing water also included the first noted nature spots in the county.

In his 1834 *Gazetteer of Illinois*, John Mason Peck asserted, "No better land can be found in Illinois than the country in general watered by this stream [Crooked Creek] and the many small tributaries emptying into it." He was promoting the area to frontier settlers as farmland, but early hunters also found it a fine place to bag ducks and geese in the spring and fall, as well as prairie chickens anytime. And the timberland near Crooked Creek and its tributaries was, and still is, good deer habitat.

But it was also well known for wolves. Those legendary predators did occasionally kill livestock, but they also symbolized the wilderness that pioneers felt they had to eliminate, so major wolf hunts were sometimes organized—and became unforgettable events. In 1904, Shadrach Campbell, then eighty years old, recalled perhaps the biggest wolf hunt in McDonough County history, held in 1843:

> *The pioneers organized for a wolf drive—to round up and exterminate the wolves if possible. Mr. Campbell was then 19 years of age and participated in the drive. Four lines were formed, the one on the west side reaching*

> *from Fandon to Blandinsville; one on the south…on the line between McDonough and Schuyler counties; one at the north line of McDonough County; and one in the western part of Fulton County. It was arranged that they…would travel to meet, driving the wolves ahead of them, and when the lines met there would be a wholesale wolf killing. The round-up came on the broad prairie about four miles east of where the courthouse stands. And in it was just one black wolf, and it got away.*

The intention was to chase the wolves from forested areas onto the expanse of prairie east of Macomb, where they could be readily shot. But as this account suggests, the wolves were not easily eliminated.

There were much smaller wolf hunts well into the 1870s. One north of Bardoph (originally called Wolf Grove) in 1874 was focused on a single wolf, which was chased across several farms near Crooked Creek and was eventually killed. Then the wolf pelt was displayed in Macomb at the county clerk's office. Shortly afterward, a large timber wolf was trapped and killed "in the neighborhood of what is known as 'wigwam hollow,'" and its hide was also placed on display in Macomb. Of course, such occasions often prompted the telling of stories about earlier wolf hunts.

As fascinating as wolves were, they were not the ultimate wild animals in McDonough County. On rare occasions a lynx or panther would be spotted and pursued. Because they were potentially dangerous to people, their very presence in the county caused public alarm. In 1867, for example, a lynx was killed northwest of Macomb, in the Spring Creek area, and as the *Eagle* reported in a headline story, "the proud hunter brought the carcass into the newspaper office, where people gazed at it with amazement," and "the presence of the animal in our city caused almost a suspension of business—everybody going to and fro wild with excitement." The six-foot lynx carcass was photographed, and several weeks later an engraved image of "the ferocious-looking and dangerous animal" was printed in the *Eagle.*

In 1873, there was a wild animal scare in southeastern McDonough County and northern Schuyler County, along Sugar Creek (another tributary of Crooked Creek), which prompted a series of folkloric stories, as the *Macomb Journal* indicated: "At first it was supposed to be a catamount [i.e., mountain lion], which in due course of time was changed to a lynx. Then…in Eldorado [Township] it grew into a pair of lynx; and in Scotland [Township] into as many panthers." Whatever it was, that animal was never killed, but stories about it circulated for years.

In 1891, a similar animal was reportedly seen on several occasions, frightening the people in Macomb Township, and it was eventually dubbed "the Crooked Creek terror." One account helps to explain why:

> *Saturday night a week ago Joe Hunt, a young son of Steve Hunt, who lives four or five miles northeast of Macomb, on Crooked Creek, while riding horseback at dark, was attacked by the Crooked Creek terror, which jumped upon the horse from a tree and injured the animal so it will likely die. It then chased boy and horse a hundred rods or more, uttering unearthly screams at every jump. The boy and his father armed themselves with the family musket and a pitchfork, and went after the animal. They found it, the musket exploded, the animal escaped into the woods, and the boy was badly powder burned….*
>
> *LATER: This week's* By-Stander *says the Crooked Creek terror was seen and heard several times last week. On Thursday night it visited Bardolph, killing two dogs and half-devouring one. Frank Spangler, a farmer living north of Bardolph, says he saw it, and that it was about five feet from tip to tip…. Several hunting parties from Macomb and Bardolph have attempted to hunt it down, without success.*

Despite the occasional stories about dangerous animals, two locations along Crooked Creek became noted for their natural beauty and were popular places for excursions and picnics. One was called Cedar Bluffs, where steep hills rose up from the little valley along the creek north of Colchester. The earliest reference to it appears in the 1871 *Macomb Journal*: "One of the most extensive fishing-picnic excursions we ever attended came off last Saturday…at Cedar Bluffs on Crooked Creek. Some fish were caught, lots of dinner masticated, and any amount of fun and enjoyment indulged in."

The newspaperman who attended that event, along with dozens of other young people, and reported on it was W.H. Hainline. In later years, he mentioned other excursions to that popular nature area, which was near the old Pleasant Valley Mill and became associated with the later recreation area at the mill site.

Another of his reports, "Wigwam Hollow: A Visit to the Yosemite of McDonough," published in 1874, refers to a similar area northwest of Macomb. Hainline points out that Asa Matteson then owned the lovely area, "composed of the valley and the environing steeps [or bluffs]," and his article also reveals that coal outcroppings there had prompted the development of a drift mine. As the years passed, "Wigwam Hollow" was used to designate the

A few Western students by the Bluffs along Crooked Creek, at Wigwam Hollow, in the early twentieth century.

valley, or flood plain, where Indians had once established a hunting camp, and the steep, picturesque spot along the north side of the river was called the Bluffs.

The coal vein proved too thin for serious mining, but that hillside remained a well-known spot for picnics during the early twentieth century. Students at Western Normal went there every year, and photographic postcards were created so they could show friends and family the noted nature spot north of the campus.

As the years passed, group excursions to both Cedar Bluffs and the Bluffs became less and less common, probably because automobiles could take people to a variety of interesting places and perhaps because the landowners near those areas did not want groups of hikers and picnickers on their property. Whatever the case, Cedar Bluffs near Colchester and the Bluffs near Macomb eventually faded from popular memory—while the nearby valleys (Pleasant Valley and Wigwam Hollow) managed to retain their identities. And fading along with those memories, over the generations, were all the nineteenth-century tales of threatening animals and exciting experiences in the wilds of Crooked Creek.